The Sino–Japanese Axis

by Dr R. Taylor

THE SINO–
JAPANESE
AXIS

A new force in Asia?

ST MARTIN'S PRESS, NEW YORK

© 1985 Robert Taylor

For information, write:
St Martin's Press, Inc.,
175 Fifth Avenue, New York, NY 10010

First published in the United States of America in 1985

ISBN 0-312-72601-5

Library of Congress Cataloging in Publication Data
Taylor, Robert, 1941–
   The Sino–Japanese axis.
   Bibliography: p.
   Includes index.
   1. Japan—Relations—China.   2. China—Relations—
Japan. I. Title.
DS849.C6T38   1985   303.4'8251'052   84-29812
ISBN 0-312-72601-5

Printed in Great Britain
by Billing & Sons Ltd, Worcester

To Ada

Contents

Preface

Diplomatic relations between the People's Republic of China and Japan were established in 1972. Since that time the world has seen a profoundly important change in the attitudes of these two countries towards one another, a change reflected in the title of this book. In prospect, it could be the most important partnership in the alignment of the great powers; a Sino–Japanese axis constituting a new force in Asia and the world at large.

On the one side there is Japan, loaded with high technology but virtually devoid of raw materials; on the other China, with an abundance of natural resources but short on technology. The circumstances, too, are propitious for such a union, given their possession of a common cultural heritage and Japan's immediate experience as one of the few successful modernizers in the non-Western world.

The first moves are already taking place. Economic and cultural interchange between the two countries has been accelerating during the last two years. An indication of this special relationship was the decision, taken during the visit to Japan in 1983 of Chinese Communist Party General Secretary, Hu Yao-bang, to establish the 21st Century Committee for Sino-Japanese Friendship, intended to promote the long-term expansion of closer political, economic and technical contacts. Subsequently, on a trip to China in March 1984, the Japanese Prime Minister, Yasuhiro Nakasone, made available a loan of two thousand million dollars to finance, over a seven-year period, crucial transportation and energy projects, the basis of China's future economic growth.

In fact, there is enormous scope for economic co-operation,

with China possessing huge untapped natural resources needed to fuel Japan's hungry industries and Japan able to supply the advanced technology so avidly sought by the Chinese to spur their country's economic growth and catch up with the advanced industrial societies of the West. A driving force in the recent expansion of Japanese steel exports has been China's accelerated investment in capital construction, and Japanese imports of Chinese oil and coal should increase in volume.

These Sino–Japanese economic ties are already creating a political alliance, promising a new balance of power in Asia within the next two decades. But both countries must move with some diplomacy to allay the suspicions of Southeast Asian governments. Such rulers remain apprehensive of China's claim to lead the forces of world revolution; nor would they regard with equanimity any attempts on the part of Japan to gain economic domination of the region at the expense of its smaller nations.

These momentous issues are the focus of this book.

Acknowledgements

I wish to thank Margaret Rotondo for typing various sections of the manuscript and Janice Mogford for preparing the index.

CHINA'S PROVINCES AND MAJOR CITIES

● Urumqi

XINJIANG

GANSU

NIN

QINGHAI Xining ●

Lanzhou ●

TIBET

Cher ●

● Lhasa

SICHUAN

GU

Kunming ●

YUNNAN

HEILONGJIANG

● Harbin

JILIN

● Changchun

INNER MONGOLIA

Shenyang
LIAONING

HEBEI   Qinhuangdao

hot ●   Beijing ●   ● Tianjin   ● Dalian
        ● Shijiazhuang

Taiyuan ●   ● Jinan
SHANXI   SHANDONG

        Zhengzhou   JIANGSU

HENAN   ANHUI   ● Nanjing

    ● Wuhan   ● Hefei   ● Shanghai

HUBEI   ZHEJIANG   ● Hangchou

    ● Nanchang

Changsha ●   JIANGXI   Fuchou ●

HUNAN   FUJIAN   ● Taipei

ANGXI   ● Guangzhou   TAIWAN

ing   ● Shenzhen (Special economic zone)
    ● Hong Kong (Brit.)
    Macao (Port.)

GUANGDONG

HAINAN   South China Sea

Yellow Sea

East China Sea

A. Bereznay

1 Introduction:
Contemporary trends

The establishment of diplomatic relations between the Chinese People's Republic and Japan during Japanese Premier Tanaka's visit to China in September 1972 placed two sovereign nations on an equal footing for the first time in their history. In earlier centuries the Japanese had never considered themselves as falling under the suzerainty of the Chinese Empire, but their country had at times been drawn into China's cultural orbit through the adoption of precepts concerning government, social status and personal morality, as well as ideographic writing. From the mid-nineteenth century to the early 1970s relations were largely conditioned by Western colonial expansion, trading interest and great-power rivalry, to which each of the two countries responded differently: China suffered political disunity, the loss of a viable central authority and infringement of sovereignty through extraterritoriality and foreign economic penetration; Japan, on the other hand, was so successful in preserving her territorial integrity and regaining tariff autonomy that it could, in the space of but a few decades, launch a policy of colonial expansion on the Asian mainland. Japanese aggression in the Second World War has proved a crucial determinant in relations between the two respective powers; invasion of China was a crucial factor in enabling the Chinese Communist Party (CCP) leaders to present themselves as a government alternative to the ruling Guomindang of Chiang Kai-shek as well as accede to power in 1949; and Japan's defeat in war, with the subsequent United States occupation of her islands, anchored Japan firmly to the Western Alliance.

On meeting Tanaka, the Chinese leader Mao Zedong

acknowledged his debt to Japan; the Chinese Communist movement was primarily nationalist, and in adapting Marxist-Leninist doctrines to local conditions it forged a new unity after decades of civil strife. In China, as elsewhere in the underdeveloped countries of the Third World, the preconditions of material abundance Marx had set for transition to socialism and ultimately Communism did not exist, and Mao sought to apply Marxist-Leninist doctrine as a means of both legitimizing his rule and achieving the goal of transforming China into an advanced industrial economy.

Thus, in view of their ideological stance and the circumstances of the Cold War, the Chinese leaders adopted the Soviet model of central economic planning as a short cut to development and China became a major outpost of international Communism. But – although Russian experts were sent to China and Chinese scientists trained in the USSR during the period of China's First Five-year Plan (1953–7) – Soviet aid, mainly in the form of loans and later repaid, proved less than generous, and by the mid-1950s there was evidence of Soviet attempts to gain direct control over the CCP.

Furthermore, Soviet planning and economic priorities had evolved in different national conditions and by the late 1950s the CCP leaders were having serious reservations about the validity of the Soviet model. The strains in the Sino–Soviet bilateral relationship were accompanied by growing disagreement over revolutionary strategy for the furtherance of Communism, especially in the Third World. The withdrawal of Soviet technicians and industrial blueprints forced the CCP leaders to make a virtue out of necessity and promote policies of national economic self-reliance; the Great Leap Forward, already under way in 1958, had been designed to achieve rapid economic growth through labour-intensive policies of local self-sufficiency rather than the tight central control associated with Soviet-type planning.

Sino–Soviet ideological differences brought traditional national animosities to the surface, as evidenced by the armed clashes on the border in 1969. During the colonial expansion of the Western powers during the mid-nineteenth century the Chinese Imperial rulers still saw their Empire as the centre of civilization and sufficient unto itself; it had no need of Western trade and they sought to restrict foreign influence by playing one power against another. Thus, in spite of foreign competition for spheres of influence in China and Soviet support for the fledgling CCP in the 1920s and 1930s and Western backing for the Guomindang, all Chinese political movements, including that of Mao Zedong – whose peasant movement eventually came to power with only minimal Soviet aid – sought to regain what they regarded as China's sovereignty, independent of alien influence. However, the Soviet leaders helped to reorganize the Guomindang on Leninist lines during the early 1920s, believing it to be China's major revolutionary force, and maintained diplomatic relations until 1949. In this sense the Sino–Soviet alliance was an aberration, forced upon the CCP leaders by the mutual misunderstandings with the United States and European powers in the years immediately before the Communist victory in 1949.

Similarly, relations with Japan were conditioned by the post-war international environment. The Sino–Soviet Treaty of Friendship, Alliance and Mutual Assistance negotiated between Stalin and Mao Zedong in February 1950 had been specifically directed against Japan or any state allied with it, implicitly the United States. But by the late 1960s the post-war bipolar world was being transformed. The territorial dimensions of the Sino–Soviet dispute were producing a Chinese reassessment of the world power balance and increasing the leadership's fears of encirclement by both superpowers, given growing United States involvement in Vietnam. But the United States, unlike the Soviet Union, was not an Asian land power, and the later American withdrawal from Vietnam was, in the Chinese view, a victory of guerrilla so-called 'People's War' over modern conventional weapons. The United States now appeared to the Chinese leaders as the weaker of the two superpowers.

In addition, significantly for later Chinese foreign policy formulation, a regional power bloc in the shape of the European Economic Community was emerging as an independent force in world politics, even if still within the framework of the Western Alliance.

Japan, like China, emerged from the Second World War in a state of economic devastation but began her process of rehabilitation under American tutelage. Japan had been reintroduced to world markets by the United States and, sheltering under the Peace Constitution of 1946 and the American defence umbrella, emerged as an economic giant in the short space of thirty years, becoming at the same time an Allied bastion against Communism in Asia. A peace treaty concluded with Chiang Kai-shek's Nationalist government on Taiwan precluded Japanese diplomatic relations with the People's Republic of China in Peking.

In this context post-war Japanese governments, since 1955 dominated by the Liberal Democratic Party, followed the guidelines of United States policy. But the unprecedented economic success of the 1960s brought a new surge of nationalistic confidence, and Japan was becoming a major export competitor of the United States. Japan, however, lacked raw materials, and exports, playing an increasing role in her economy, were crucially necessary for survival in a highly competitive world market. Thus during the 1960s and 1970s Japan's diplomacy remained omnidirectional, that is, adjusting to changes in the international environment and seeking economic relationships with all countries regardless of ideology, being reluctant to offend potential suppliers and customers. Japanese policy nevertheless remained within the overall framework of the United States alliance.

Ever since the 1950s, however, certain sections of Japanese society, and not exclusively the left of the political spectrum, had been distinctly unhappy with successive governments' China policy. There had been the formation of a pro-Peking faction in the ruling Liberal Democratic Party, called the Asian-African Problems Research Association, in 1965 and in 1970 379 Diet (parliament) members from all the major parties joined forces to organize the super-partisan Dietmen's League for the Restoration of Ties with China,[1] attempting to mobilize all forces, including business, to exert pressure on the government. There had always been strong support among Japanese voters for recognition of the Peking regime.[2]

The United States *rapprochement* with China, symbolized by

President Nixon's meeting with the Chinese leader Mao Zedong in Peking in February 1972, provided the necessary impetus for a change in Japanese China policy. Initially taken by surprise, sections of Japan's business establishment, fearing that the United States would now be given a flying start in the race for the China trade hitherto restricted by the American strategic embargo, pressed for immediate recognition of the People's Republic of China. But an independent initiative seemed problematical, especially in view of the stance of the Sato cabinet, which had always been too closely identified with the previous American anti-Communist hard line in Asia. But divisions within the ruling party of government, the Liberal Democrats, had always provided flexibility for policy manoeuvre, and the accession to power of Tanaka and his powerful faction, endorsed by the electorate in July 1972, paved the way for the normalization of Sino–Japanese relations in September of the same year, thus placing the seal of legitimacy on growing economic and political links between the two countries.

Constraints were also being lifted on the Chinese side as the habitual attacks in the Party press began to give way to a more sober reappraisal of the role Japan might play in the defence of Asia and the Pacific, especially in the wake of United States withdrawal from Vietnam and a growing Soviet naval presence in the Indian Ocean. Having previously castigated United States imperialism in the region, the Chinese now feared that the Soviet Union would fill the vacuum, with results detrimental to China's security interests.

Redefinition of Japan's role will therefore be seen in the context of the reformulation of Chinese foreign policy in the early 1970s, as expressed in the 'three worlds' theory which reflected Chinese perceptions of a new world power balance. As in the case of the Sino–Japanese relationship, the new doctrinal pronouncement on foreign policy came long after relevant changes were already in effect. In 1964, with the burgeoning of the Sino–Soviet dispute and the disintegration of the two world power blocs, Mao Zedong had elaborated the concept of the second intermediate zone, suggesting the idea of a united front between China and those whom he regarded as its lesser enemies – like the industrialized countries of Western Europe together with Japan – against major enemies, the United States and so-called Soviet social imperialism which, in the CCP's view, was even more pernicious, having betrayed the cause of world revolution through failure to support the national liberation struggles in the Third World, and policies of social inequality at home.

The 'second intermediate' idea was a prelude to Mao Zedong's articulation of the 'three worlds' concept, given further explicit and public expression in a speech by the newly rehabilitated Deng Xiaoping, who had been disgraced in the Cultural Revolution of the late 1960s, to the United Nations General Assembly in April 1974. Deng stated that the socialist camp, formerly led by the Soviet Union, had now ceased to exist. By extension, the world was divided into three parts, with the superpowers, the United States and the Soviet Union, making up the first world; the developing countries of Asia, Africa, and Latin America forming the third; and the developed countries of Western Europe and Japan being the second.

By 1975 it was clear that this doctrinal formulation was intended to promote a global anti-hegemony united front against the Soviet Union, and in subsequent years it underwent further redefinition. Fewer references were made to the United States as an imperialist power, as the Chinese leaders had come to regard it as belonging to the second world rather than the first. The United States was thereby perceived as a developed capitalist country which, like the former imperialist powers of Western Europe, had waned in power and influence, being forced to abandon its hopes of world domination.[3]

Moreover, in 1982 the *People's Daily*, the leading media organ of the CCP, explained how the relationship between a militarily offensive Soviet Union and a militarily defensive United States was having worldwide repercussions. According to this view, the major Soviet aim was to seize strategic positions, resources and communication routes; simultaneously, attempts were in motion to wreck the Western Alliance and force the countries of the European Economic Community (EEC) to take a neutral position between the superpowers. Meanwhile, through Soviet penetration of the Third World, the influence of the West as a whole would be reduced.[4]

These definitive statements would appear to rule out any possibility of Sino–Soviet reconciliation in the foreseeable future. But in late 1982 and the beginning of 1983 there were nevertheless signs of an easing of tension between the two Communist giants, as the Chinese leaders proclaimed the need to keep channels of communication open while repeating the view that Soviet hegemony still constituted the main threat to world peace. Thus, if the bitter ideological dispute has been toned down in recent years with the Chinese ceasing to attack Soviet domestic doctrine and policy as well as accepting the need for each society to develop according to its own conditions, national rivalry between the two powers remains. The Chinese leaders themselves have readily admitted that there still exist major obstacles to the improvement of Sino–Soviet relations; the Soviet Union continues to intervene in Afghanistan, to support Vietnamese action in Cambodia and to deploy a million troops along the frontier between the two countries.

China's moves may well be an attempt to reassert an independent foreign policy stance and gain as much leverage as possible in the international balance of power. To domestic critics, for example, Deng Xiaoping and his supporters seem to have made little headway concerning the problem of Taiwan. China claims sovereignty over the island, the Nationalist government of which is still receiving American military aid. Equable relations with both the Soviet Union and the United States are thus designed to placate fundamentalist left-wing opinion in China among top army commanders and high provincial administrators opposed to the current leadership by removing any threats of domination by either of the superpowers.

There seems little chance, then, of China returning to the Soviet fold as a committed ally; but it is equally unlikely that China will be able to match the military power of the Soviet Union for some decades to come, even with recent United States sales of civil aircraft to China and Sino-American collaboration in anti-Soviet surveillance. Increasing China's military capability could, however, bring nearer the likelihood of Chinese aggression against Vietnam or Taiwan.[5] While limited forms of military and economic co-operation may be in the West's interest, too great a use of the China card could be seen as a serious threat by the Soviet Union. On the other side, attempts by China and the Soviet Union to take the heat out of the national dispute may make the latter less sensitive concerning Western aid for China's modernization pro-gramme.[6] The Chinese leaders seek to rally as many forces as possible by forming a wide international united front against the superpowers. They see their country as having fewer contentious issues and greater community of interest with Japan and the EEC than with the United States. But however disappointed the Chinese may have been over their relations with the Americans, they are at pains to deny that new moves towards Sino–Soviet *détente* will affect China's commitment to economic and technical co-operation with the West.[7]

In their conviction that the key to China's national security lies in alliance with the second, and to a lesser extent the Third World, the CCP leaders have sought to convince the countries of the EEC and Japan of the need to counter Soviet global strategy. Thus, in the Chinese view, attention is focused on technologically advanced and materially wealthy Europe, the crucial factor in Soviet contention with the United States for world supremacy, because of its heavy concentration of military forces and weapons. Similarly, the United States has always made Europe its strategic focus.

At the same time, however, the Soviet leaders aim to strengthen the Eastern front, eliminating United States influ-ence from Asia and the Pacific as well as preventing an alliance between China, Japan and America. They therefore have an interest in thwarting any strategic relationship between Western Europe and China, encouraging the for-mer's peace movement and detaching NATO countries from the American connection. With the EEC countries neutralized, the Soviet leadership would have a free hand to acquire the wealth of Western Europe and extend their hegemony over the Asian mainland as well as the Pacific. Any attempts by

EEC countries to co-ordinate their foreign and security policies and realize the full implications of the Treaty of Rome are seized upon with alacrity by Chinese commentators, as are the activities of the non-governmental international organization the Trilateral Commission, which consists of influential personages and is designed to foster political and economic co-operation among the industrialized countries of North America, Western Europe, and Japan.[8]

Until the end of the 1970s there was a latent conflict between China's growing links with Western European countries and her aspirations to lead the developing states of Asia, Africa and Latin America. But gradually Chinese policy towards the Third World underwent a change of emphasis. In the 1950s and 1960s the Chinese had promoted, morally and sometimes materially, national liberation movements in the developing countries; in the 1970s they began to support, especially after the admission of the People's Republic to the United Nations, Third World demands for a new international economic order and, specifically, better terms of trade with the West. In addition, ever since 1949 the CCP had disseminated its own model of social and economic change for adoption by Third World countries. In 1978, however, the Chinese began to subordinate their Third World policy to the creation of an international united front against the Soviet Union. Consequently, calls for a new international economic order took second place to a concern with the alleged Soviet political and military threat to the sovereignty of developing countries, and the Chinese downplayed their former domestic policies as a model of development in the Third World.[9] With this change of emphasis came a less rigorous analysis of the internal class structure in developing countries; alleged Soviet stress on the paramount importance of class struggle in such states was described as an attempt to capitalize on local conflicts, thereby promoting Soviet interests at the expense of Third World countries.[10] In addition, in wooing Third World countries as anti-Soviet allies, the Chinese refuse to give weight to divisions in the developing world between, for example, oil-exporting and oil-importing states.[11] In similar vein, the *Beijing Review* commented favourably on what it called EEC attempts to improve relations with Third World countries on the basis of mutual respect for sovereignty and equality; Foreign Minister Huang Hua, in an address to the Council of Europe Parliamentary Assembly, praised West European efforts in helping the Third World to promote development and stability.[12]

Thus, while the Chinese leaders still retain their belief in world revolution and the ultimate triumph of Communism worldwide in the long term, political alliance with the former so-called Imperialist countries of the 'second world' and the incumbent governments of the Third World, whatever their political complexion, will remain the basic concern of Chinese foreign policy in coming decades. Too close an alignment with the Western powers would, however, reduce China's credibility in the eyes of the Third World; Premier Zhao Ziyang's 1983 visit to eleven African countries was an attempt to demonstrate that China's current practice of Realpolitik and aspiration to world-power status did not in any way mean abandonment of China's support for the cause of the developing countries.

But the EEC countries and Japan offer China a greater source of political, military and economic co-operation than does the Third World, and Chinese leaders would be reluctant to place undue reliance on their relationship with the United States in view of their country's exclusive ties with the Soviet Union in the 1950s. Nevertheless, given China's foreign policy reorientation, it is necessary to assess the extent to which her leaders' views of the 'second world' are reciprocated by Japan and Western Europe.

Since the end of the United States Occupation in 1952, the Japanese have pursued an economic foreign policy and omni-directional diplomacy, albeit within the framework of the American alliance. They were anxious to sign the Peace Treaty with China in 1978 but reluctant to subscribe fully to Chinese views on Soviet 'hegemony'. Certainly Article II of the Treaty, in which the contracting parties declared that 'neither of them should seek hegemony in the Asia-Pacific region or any other region and that each is opposed to efforts by any other country or group of countries to establish such hegemony', the latter phrase being implicit reference to the Soviet Union, represented a limited concession to the Chinese view. But the Japanese nevertheless managed to weaken the force of the clause by including the phrase 'any other region'; additionally, in suggesting the general 'each country is opposed to' rather than the specific 'each country will oppose', the Japanese absolved themselves from the responsibility to take joint action with China in the event of hegemonism by a third country. Similarly, Japan's desire for omnidirectional diplomacy was reflected in Article IV, which stated that 'the present treaty shall not affect the position of either contracting party regarding its relations with third countries'.[13]

Successive Japanese governments have nevertheless shared Chinese apprehension concerning the Soviet military build-up in Northeast Asia. In July 1981 Mr Joji Omura, Director-General of the Japanese Defence Agency, speaking to a parliamentary committee in the Diet, referred to the need for Japan to improve its defence capabilities in the face of the Soviet Union's growing military strength in the region.[14] Consequently, Japan has been responding more readily to American arguments that Japan play a greater role in the defence of Asia; in early October 1982 United States government sources were confirming plans to base 50 F 16 fighters at Misawa Air Base in Northern Japan.

This policy has been in response to the deployment of new Soviet warships, the latter being specifically designed not only to provide a naval and air screen for the Sea of Okhotsk but to increase the capabilities of the Pacific Fleet for sustained operation in the South China Sea and the Indian Ocean. While both China and Japan are apprehensive about Soviet naval potential in Southeast Asia, Japan's immediate concern is Soviet air patrols over and near the Kurile islands, territories currently in dispute between Japan and the Soviet Union.[15]

Ever since the establishment of diplomatic relations between the two countries in 1956, the Japanese have consistently declined to sign a peace treaty with the Soviet Union until the territorial issue is resolved. The Japanese claim two of the disputed islands as an integral part of Hokkaido, while the Southern Kuriles were not included in the lands renounced by Japan under the San Francisco Peace Treaty of 1952. There are two considerations in the Soviet refusal to give up the islands: first, they are invaluable for surveillance of the American and Japanese defence manoeuvres and installations and secondly, revision of the boundaries with Japan would set a dangerous precedent, making the Russians vulnerable to claims for territorial concessions in Europe and, perhaps more significantly, from China.

The Chinese have sought to capitalize on this territorial issue, castigating the Soviet leaders as inheritors of the mantle of the 'Imperialist Tsars'. On 7 February 1981 the *People's Daily* commemorated the newly instituted 'Japanese Northern Territories Day' by upholding 'the just struggle of the Japanese people'.

In addition, although not subscribing fully to the Chinese view of the global strategic situation, the Japanese have demanded and received assurances from the Americans that any future agreement between the United States and the Soviet Union on reducing medium-range missiles in Europe will not be at the expense of Asian interests; Japan's fear is that Russian SS-20 missiles pulled out of Europe could be redeployed in the East. This view was echoed by Li Luye, the Chinese delegate to the forty-nation United Nations Disarmament Committee in Geneva, who referred to the possibility of some of the mobile SS-20s being moved from Europe to the Sino–Soviet border.[16]

But, in spite of such areas of agreement, recent developments have indicated that the Japanese are not prepared to sacrifice their national interests for the sake of their relationship with China. In May 1980, for example, the *Beijing Review* described the Japanese–South Korean Agreement to co-operate in oil-drilling on the East China Sea continental shelf as null and void on the grounds that China had not been consulted on the demarcation of the territorial waters in question.[17] Likewise, the Chinese protested in July 1981 at a Japanese fisheries survey of the Diaoyutai Islands, situated northeast of Taiwan and claimed by both China and Japan.

Another instance suggests that the Japanese are not always

well attuned to Chinese sensibilities. In mid-1982 the Japanese Education Ministry produced a controversial version of Japan's twentieth-century role in China, with revisions changing Japan's 'aggression against China' into its 'advance into China' and eliminating previous references to the deaths of 200,000 in the wartime capital of Nanking.[18] This was in contrast with Japan's officially expressed repentance for wartime atrocities offered and accepted during the establishment of diplomatic relations in 1972.[19]

Whatever concessions the Japanese may have made in the textbook dispute, China remains but one factor in Japan's foreign policy thinking. Moreover, the Japanese have too great an economic stake, especially in relations with the Soviet Union, to subscribe fully to China's view of the world. Since the 1970s the Japanese have been aiding Siberian development. Japan imports nearly all her energy and raw materials and, ever conscious of the vulnerability of oil supplies from the Middle East, successive governments have sought alternative supplies closer at hand, albeit with a long-term perspective. To this end, the Export-Import Bank concluded an agreement in December 1981 to provide the Soviet Union with US$900 million in low-interest loans to help finance coal and forestry development projects in Siberia. The same bank had already extended US$450 million in loans to the Soviet Union to finance the Siberian coal project begun in 1974. In return, the Japanese are expected to receive about 100 million tons of coal from the Soviet Union over the next twenty years. The Siberian forestry development project is expected to supply Japan with 15 million cubic feet of timber over the next five years. Additionally, Nippon Steel and other companies have been involved in supplying the Soviet Union with pipes for the Siberian gas project.

Most EEC countries, like Japan, share a defence commitment with the United States, but they do not see this as precluding limited *détente* and economic co-operation with the Soviet Union. The Chinese leaders, in contrast, while not ruling out the desirability of arms limitation talks in Europe, consider *détente* as a smokescreen. Thus, even though the Chinese have confirmed their approval of Western Europe's assertive independence in a multi-polar world, they have frequently warned against exchanging independence from the United States for *détente* with the Soviet Union.[20]

There is, too, a sense in which the Chinese make common cause with the United States in urging NATO countries to take a greater share in the defence of Western interests in such areas as Asia, Africa and the Middle East. France and West Germany were criticized for failing to realize fully the grave implications of the Soviet invasion of Afghanistan.[21]

But, like the Japanese, West European countries have sheltered under a United States nuclear umbrella while simultaneously pursuing economic co-operation with the Soviet Union, as exemplified by determination to pursue the gas pipeline project with Russia, even in the face of short-term American opposition. Allied commitment to resist Soviet armed might in Europe does not preclude giving the Soviet Union an economic stake in the *status quo*. Soviet energy will, in any case, represent only a percentage of, for example, West Germany's future needs.

If China's current relations with both Japan and the EEC countries rule out any form of political and military alliance, various kinds of defence and economic ties are nevertheless proving mutually advantageous. Both China and the EEC countries seek new markets and sources of supply; for the former, such ties obviate the necessity of any excessive reliance on the United States. Furthermore, the Chinese may well profit from rivalry within the EEC; in spite of an expressed desire for ultimate political union, individual countries vary in their attitudes to such issues as free trade.

The question of military co-operation between China and the 'second world' must be viewed within two perspectives: (1) China's defence policy and (2) relations between the great powers in Asia. In spite of dissident voices within the Chinese military, some of whom are disappointed at the low priority accorded to weapons procurements and technical improvement of the armed forces, the current political leadership place their faith in economic development as the best guarantee of national defence.[22] This thesis, in suggesting China's need for a peaceful international environment as a prerequisite for successful modernization, does not preclude limited arms purchases. Her considerable nuclear arsenal notwithstanding, China's conventional weapons are mostly obsolete versions of Soviet 1950s technology.

In November 1982 Britain signed a contract worth an estimated £100 million for the sale of arms to China. The agreement, the first with a Western country, provided for the purchase of Sea Dart missiles, radar and electronic equipment, in addition to the refitting of Chinese naval destroyers.[23] Although this deal was later cancelled, it does indicate the direction of Chinese defence planning. The signs are that China's navy, until recently of value only for coastal defence, will soon have major war potential in East Asian waters.

It seems unlikely, however, that the Chinese will rely exclusively on one source for modernization of the defence forces; negotiations in the 1980s have indicated the Chinese leaders' intention to divide procurement sectors among various EEC countries. Rivalry among such Western powers – including the United States, with its lifting of the former strategic embargo against China – will be intense because they fear that eventually the Japanese will change their 'peace Constitution' of 1946, which still prevents Japan from exporting arms.

In the long term, however, Japan has a potential advantage over the EEC states; it is more directly involved, as is China, in the general security of Asia or, more specifically, resistance to the threat posed by Soviet influence and armed might. An examination of Japan's defence expenditure and armed strength will provide the background against which possible Sino–Japanese collaboration may be viewed.

The 1946 Constitution, imposed upon a defeated Japan by the United States, forbade the development of offensive military capability. But with the development of the Cold War American policy-makers, seeing Japan as an allied bastion against Communism in Asia, encouraged the formation of the euphemistically named Self-Defence Forces, interpreted as falling within the spirit of that Constitution, which they said granted Japan, in common with all countries, the inherent right of self-defence. Nevertheless, in pursuing an economic foreign policy, successive Japanese governments have forbidden the despatch of troops overseas and limited defence spending to 1 per cent of GNP.

But the continuing health of the Japanese economy, even in the face of the world recession, has brought American pressures for Japan to play a greater role in the defence of Asia.

In December 1982, responding both to demands of Western allies and increasing Soviet military activities in Northeast Asia, the Nakasone cabinet adopted a 1983 budget which increased defence spending by 6.5 per cent by forcing through cuts in social programmes.[24] Japan's potential is perhaps best indicated by her growing self-reliance in the production of munitions and military hardware such as aircraft, tanks and warships; negotiations are now afoot to allow American arms manufacturers to acquire Japanese weapons technology.

In addition, Japan's Defence Agency disclosed in 1982 that it was developing a surface-to-surface missile, expected to be ready for deployment in 1988 and powerful enough to reach the Soviet territory of Sakhalin and the disputed islands of Kunashiri and Shikotan, thus bringing into focus the thin line between offensive and defensive capability.[25]

Certainly there is greater acceptance of increased military spending in Japan, but this enhanced defence potential does not of itself mean that the Japanese are willing or able to undertake further commitments in Asia. In spite of Premier Nakasone's pledge that his country would play a greater military role in Northeast Asia, evidence to date suggests that defence is conceived of in terms of the Japanese islands and their immediate environs, up to a distance of 1000 nautical miles. Moreover, land-based Japanese air defence forces do not have the necessary range because the Constitution limits them to defensive action over their homeland; consequently, in the event of hostilities, Japanese ships would lack adequate air cover.[26] The implication is that the Japanese might handle the initial brunt of an attack, but offensive action beyond the range of Japanese capabilities would activate the Defence Treaty with the United States and bring into play American air power.

Japan is in any case the major power most vulnerable to

economic blockade, and the basic concern of any Japanese government is a defence and foreign policy directed at ensuring the safe passage of raw material imports. With regard to Northeast Asia, Japanese and Chinese perceptions of the Soviet threat may coincide, but in the case of Southeast Asia the notion that economic stability guarantees political stability has been crucial to Japanese policy thinking. Accordingly, the Japanese have urged the Chinese leaders to improve relations with the non-Communist governments of ASEAN countries by abjuring support for the Communist parties and insurrectionary movements of the region.

Thus any military co-operation between China and Japan will very likely be limited to the visits by high-ranking military officers and the exchange of information called for by Song Zhiguang, the new Chinese ambassador to Japan, in February 1982.[27]

To date, however, such exchanges have not been as numerous as consultations between the ranking military officers of West European countries and their Chinese counterparts.

In fact, China's immediate priorities are mainly economic and it is here that scope for co-operation with the countries of the 'second world' is greatest. At the Fourth National People's Congress, a session of China's parliament, in January 1975 Zhou Enlai endorsed an activist trade policy. As in the case of the 'three worlds' theory, however, the doctrinal formulation legitimized changes already taking place. Even during the self-reliance phase of the early 1960s – a policy necessitated by the withdrawal of Soviet assistance – technology purchases from abroad were being accorded an important role in China's development programme, even though such imports were then designed to supplement rather than replace indigenous development.[28] The so-called 'moderate' position, associated with Zhou Enlai and his protégé Deng Xiaoping, was as yet not fully accepted within the CCP leadership; in an address to the UN General Assembly in 1974 Deng had countered the charges of the radicals that economic contacts made China susceptible to foreign economic exploitation, and stress on equitably based overseas exchanges continued even during growing leftist influence in China during 1975.[29] Since the arrest of the leading radical, Mao's widow Jiang Qing, and her major supporters shortly after Mao's death in 1976, strengthened economic ties with the West have been confirmed, in spite of readjustment in Chinese domestic economic policy targets, and, barring major internal political upheaval, are likely to continue in some form during coming decades.

Western businessmen have taken great comfort from the outward-looking policies of China's current leadership: their forebears also saw the Chinese Empire as a vast El Dorado of wealth waiting to be tapped during the middle years of the nineteenth century. In the long run their optimism may well be justified, but in the short term the China market has undoubted limitations. Although China's foreign trade increased rapidly after the Cultural Revolution – from US$3860 million in 1969 to US$14,090 million in 1975 – in the early 1980s imports and exports together amounted to only about 4 to 5 per cent of her GNP and represented merely around 1 per cent of total world commerce, as compared with equivalent figures of 10.9 per cent for the United States, 10.5 per cent for West Germany, and 6.3 per cent in the case of Japan.[30] In addition, China was incurring deficits unprecedented in her post-1949 trading relations; these amounted to US$1100 million in 1974[31] and US$3000 million in 1980.

Deficits indicate China's growing dependence on Western, especially United States, technology to develop her physical infrastructure and industry. In view of the Chinese leaders' wish to adopt an equidistant stance between the two superpowers the Japanese, who have acquired and then adapted United States technology in, for example, the field of oil-prospecting and drilling equipment, are ideally placed to aid China in the exploitation of natural resources through equipment sales and economic co-operation. Furthermore it will take time for China's economy, originally modelled on Soviet central planning, to be incorporated into the mechanisms of capitalism and the international system, and the Japanese have been showing increasing interest in playing a mediating role in this process, as witnessed by the then Foreign Minister Sunao Sonoda's statement to the Japan Society in New York in September 1981.[32]

China's Western orientation has been reflected in the changing geographical pattern of her world trade. Even before foreign policy reformulation in the 1970s, the Chinese were diversifying their sources of supply with increasing plant and technology imports from Japan and Western Europe. These trends, of course, continued in the next decade; during the period 1970–78 Japan was China's single most important partner, providing 28 per cent of her imports including mainly metals, machinery, and equipment, and taking 18 per cent of her exports, mainly oil. The countries of Western Europe supplied 23 per cent of China's imports, predominantly industrial supplies and capital goods, and bought 13 per cent of her exports, mostly manufactures and raw materials.[33] By 1980 Sino–Japanese trade totalled over US$9 billion, increasing to over 10 billion the following year.[34]

There are, however, weaknesses in the commodity structure of China's foreign trade, biased as it is towards intensive light industrial goods; in 1982, for example, out of a total of $2 billion-worth of Chinese goods exported to the United States, textiles were valued at US$800 million.[35] In a world context China relies on textile exports for nearly a fourth of her foreign exchange earnings.[36] But by early 1983 Chinese exports were encountering growing calls for protectionism from United States domestic producers, as well as competition from such Third World countries as the states of Southeast Asia. But, although the proportion of manufactured goods in China's total exports rose, for instance, from 49.7 per cent in 1980 to 53.4 per cent in 1981, this category also includes such goods as machine tools and metal industry products which may, in the short term, be subject to less rigorous competition.[37]

Nevertheless, export competitiveness is only one factor in China's economic health. Even with the institution of rigorous birth-control policies, permitting one child per family, agricultural yields are failing to keep pace with population growth and economic performance still depends to a large extent on the previous year's harvest.

Thus during the period 1970–78 foodstuffs accounted for 15 per cent of China's imports and, while the proportion of manufactured goods to total purchases abroad fell from 65.1

per cent in 1980 to 63.4 per cent in 1981, the percentage of primary products rose from 34.9 in 1980 to 36.6 the following year.[38] Grain purchases from the West will clearly remain considerable.

But grain imports, like the food aid provided by the EEC and Japan during the natural disasters of early 1981, can be only temporary palliatives, and the key to China's prosperity lies in developing her agricultural and other natural resources through the acquisition of technological knowhow and investment. To this end China joined the International Monetary Fund (IMF) and the World Bank in the spring of 1980, but Japan and the EEC will remain crucial sources of technical knowledge and equipment for the exploitation of vast untapped reserves of oil, coal and non-ferrous metals. The creation of a modern transport and communications infrastructure, as well as the construction of chemical fertilizer plants, will similarly benefit from the expertise of the 'second world'. Although China will continue to import grain for the foreseeable future, the advanced economies have much to offer in the field of agricultural research; Japanese experts have already helped to increase yields in Southeast Asian countries.

In spite of Japan's aid commitments elsewhere in Asia and the sensitivity of some countries in the region to any increase in Chinese economic strength and political influence, Japanese ruling circles believe their country has a considerable stake in China's development and are prepared to take short-term risks for long-term economic advantage. The Japanese see economic growth as a key to the survival of the current moderate Chinese leadership and, ultimately, the creation of political stability. Notable examples of China's acceptance of assistance from Japan have been a fiscal 1979 yen credit from the Overseas Economic Co-operation Fund (OECF) at 3 per cent interest, repayable over thirty years with a ten-year grace period, and a similar arrangement for 1980 on equally lenient terms.[39] Likewise, loans have been contracted with the IMF and the countries of the EEC.

Recent diplomatic exchanges suggest that the Chinese reciprocate Japanese optimism concerning economic co-operation; in his above-quoted statement of February 1982 the new Chinese envoy to Japan spoke of better prospects for China's relations with Japan than with Western Europe. The two economies could prove complementary, as China's natural resources fuel Japan's modern economy with energy and raw materials. Moreover in time, as China's economy advances, it could become a market for those Japanese goods now increasingly facing protectionist measures in Western Europe and the United States. There are also the intangibles of a common cultural heritage; as one of the few non-Western countries to modernize Japan is well placed to be a mediator of those values, or philosophical infrastructure, underpinning an advanced industrial society.

2 Philosophical Infrastructure: Japan as mentor

In dedicating themselves to the task of modernization China's leaders, like their counterparts elsewhere in the Third World, have sought historical precedents to guide their development programme. Japan, as one of the few non-Western countries to modernize and with a shared cultural heritage, seems a natural choice; nations, like individuals, however, have a unique personal style determining pace and stage of growth at a particular point in time, and accelerated technological advance in the contemporary world in any case precludes the exact reproduction of another country's development process. China's society and economy, then, can never be carbon copies of Japan, but certain lessons may nevertheless be drawn from Japan's experience, and the Japanese may help the Chinese to create the kind of social climate most conducive to economic success.

This social climate may be better defined as the philosophical infrastructure, the fostering of those institutions and values characteristic of the advanced industrial societies of the West. A cursory examination of both countries' reaction to the impact of Western technological and economic power in the mid-nineteenth century suggests that there are as yet formidable cultural as well as political and institutional barriers to be overcome before relevant lessons of the Japanese experience may be learned.

Modernization is not merely a question of establishing new political and economic institutions but demands the inculcation of values; institutions certainly create values and yet also reflect them. Unlike China, Japan had a long tradition of cultural borrowing, thus possessing certain attributes favourable to modernization. The Confucian ethic – like the Chinese written language, adopted early in Japanese history – was given a unique Japanese cast. Moreover, knowledge was more practically oriented than in China, and this enabled the populace at large to accept more readily the need for science and technology to strengthen their country against the onslaught of the West. Because of its rapid response to the demands of a new age, the old social and political order was never completely discredited: in Meiji Japan the survival of traditional values made possible social cohesion and national integration; the old virtues and a precedent for cultural borrowing legitimized the input of foreign technology, with Western now being substituted for rejected aspects of Chinese learning. In turn, continuity of social values and the acceptance of foreign knowledge formed a secure base for the next stage of adjustment to the West, as Japan's leaders realized that the commercial and military supremacy of the Occident was a product of specific cultural values underpinning political institutions and education systems.

In their attempts to regain and then strengthen national sovereignty, such leaders were careful to choose those models best suited to the authoritarian traditions of Japanese society and the economic development goals of the ruling oligarchy: witness the adoption of a Prussian-style constitution and the establishment of a French-type highly centralized education system. Japanese Society, however, like all societies, has proved dynamic. Moreover its history has been cyclical, with periods of cultural and technological assimilation followed by the reassertion of native tradition, resulting in a unique blend of old and new. Ultimately, the adoption of Western ways for self-defence stimulated an aggressive Japanese nationalism.

In China, traditional social values precluded the full utilization of considerable centuries-old scientific invention, and no industrial revolution took place. Nor – unlike Japan's – was the social climate receptive to the absorption of foreign technology. On the contrary, mid-nineteenth-century Chinese reformers failed to see the inevitable interaction between institutions and values, believing that technical progress from abroad could easily be grafted on to China's traditional political and social system. To the extent that China has not yet fully modernized she is still responding to the impact of Western civilization.

If Chinese reformers had not yet concluded that the material strength of Western countries lay in their political institutions and philosophy, they nevertheless saw the need to send students abroad, especially to Japan and Europe. Thus by the late nineteenth century a precedent was being set for Japanese participation in China's development, with a reversal of historical roles.

Qing dynasty officials were impressed by Meiji achievements and Chinese students, newly returned from study in Japan, were already playing prominent roles in government, education, commerce and industry by the early years of the twentieth century. Similarly, Japanese advisers and teachers aided China's early modernization efforts.

Although, ultimately, such Japanese assistance was not entirely disinterested – leading as it did to the military aggression of the 1930s – the students who returned to China from Japan helped to forge a sense of Chinese nationalism, just as traditional élites in the post-1945 Third World have been inspired, by the political ideals of metropolitan European countries, to form independence movements in Asia and Africa.

National independence and economic development can, however, be guaranteed only if the existing political order is seen as legitimate in the eyes of the governed. In the mid-nineteenth century the Chinese and the Japanese had differing conceptions of the Imperial institution, their focus of national loyalty. The Chinese Emperor justified his position by personal performance, and his Mandate of Heaven could be withdrawn by an aggrieved populace if his rule were seen as unjust or incompetent; the Emperor of Japan, on the other hand, owed his position to succession and, not being involved in the day-to-day conduct of government, was less accountable to the popular will. This conception of the Imperial institution gave the Japanese undoubted advantages over China in their search for new viable authority structures to retain sovereignty in the face of Western encroachment.

During the two centuries prior to the Meiji Restoration of 1868 Japan was divided into a number of fiefdoms, or domains, governed by lords who owed allegiance to a central authority, the Shogun, a kind of regent who ruled in the Emperor's name. Thus the Japanese Emperor performed only the ceremonial functions of kingship, and when the Shogun failed to provide effective leadership in the face of Western demands for trade and treaties, the Imperial institution remained sacrosanct. The new rulers, the Meiji oligarchy, drawn from *Samurai* of the southern and western domains, then held power in the name of the Emperor, who legitimized their regime, ensuring social cohesion and a focus of national loyalty. The Emperor thus became a symbol around which the nation could rally in the face of the foreign threat.

The Chinese Emperor, in contrast, ruled as well as reigned, and his legitimacy was called into question once the governmental system had been discredited through the Imperial ruler's failure to resist Western military might; from the fall of the last dynasty, the Qing, in 1911 until the creation of viable authority patterns with the Communist accession in 1949, all political movements sought a new ideological synthesis to encompass the twin demands of nationalism and modernization.

Nevertheless, however effective the Imperial institution may have been in forging a sense of national unity in Japan after 1868, it was during the two centuries of internal peace from the Tokugawa unification to the Meiji Restoration that the philosophical infrastructure of modernization was being laid.

In earlier centuries Japan had only tenuous diplomatic and commercial relations with China, but adopted the Chinese social status system. Japan, however, unlike China, elevated the position of the soldier, the *Samurai*; and a feudalism, like that of Europe, based rank on landholding. Moreover, for centuries Japan's rulers had imposed a policy of national seclusion and this, simultaneous with a long period of internal peace, produced socio-economic change and the evolution of institutions analogous to those emerging in early modern Europe before the industrial revolution. In practice, the

Samurai increasingly abandoned their military function and became specialist administrators in the castle towns. They were now virtually salaried officials; although they still nominally derived income from land, they neither owned it nor controlled those working it. Furthermore, their horizons widened as they travelled on behalf of their feudal lords to Edo, the Bakufu capital, and more significantly to Nagasaki, through which trade with the Dutch had been traditionally permitted and where *Samurai* became more exposed to Western ideas. In turn, a slackening of personal discipline in the absence of armed combat permitted a luxurious life-style beyond their means. This resulted in a growing indebtedness to a rising class of entrepreneurs, the merchants, and the newly forged link between these two groups formed the basis of co-operation between the state bureaucracy and business after the Meiji Restoration of 1868.

This increased commercial activity and the growth of a money economy were made possible by traditional Japanese social values, and in turn themselves fostered new attitudes. Unlike China, where the early abolition of primogeniture forced the division of land among several sons, in Japan the system of a single heir permitted the accumulation of family wealth in the countryside and this, in conjunction with a tradition of saving rather than increased consumption, provided a crucial source of investment in, for example, small industrial enterprises. Economic development was also assisted by the traditional subordination of the individual to the group. Rarely have individual interests been seen as legitimate in Japan, unless couched in terms of a wider interest, and individuals have drawn emotional security from total loyalty to an organization. When, for instance, migrants left their family or village in the late nineteenth and early twentieth centuries to seek their fortune in the cities they were not expected to return, and had every incentive to acquire those technical skills necessary to promote the interests and competitive position of the new enterprises they had joined. Traditional social values were thus perpetuated in a new form, and such commitments could be extended to regional and national loyalties as the horizons of individual Japanese widened in the wake of increased communication and indus-trialization.[1] Similarly, successful businessmen, unlike their Chinese counterparts, did not seek to place the seal of respectability on their newly acquired wealth by investing in land but spurred the nation's economic progress by putting it to work in new, more productive secondary industries.[2]

While the increasing complexity of economic and political institutions began to foster new public attitudes conducive to national development, new technical expertise, following greater division of labour in the industrialization process, demanded the training of a skilled labour force. Even before the Meiji oligarchs had taken steps to encourage occupational mobility among all social classes, the principle of merit was gaining support among reformers towards the end of the Tokugawa period. As the control of the central government, the Bakufu, weakened in the face of Western demands for concessions, domain leaders had greater opportunity to con-solidate their own power through the employment of better-educated officials.

Initially, education had been for the élite: the Shogun established schools in Edo for training officials, and the feudal lords sought to educate the sons of their *Samurai*. But any injunctions against commoners receiving education were not uniformly enforced; by the late Tokugawa period household heads in the countryside, and many merchants in the towns, had acquired basic literacy and numeracy skills as well as moral training through the Confucian classics, with instruc-tion being given a practical bent, addressed to the problems of measurement and accounting in everyday life.[3] So great was the desire for knowledge as society grew more complex, that by the end of the Tokugawa period there were about 17,000 schools of all kinds, including Shogunal and fief institutions, private schools which taught pupils predominantly from the merchant classes, and the Terakoya or village schools. Some-times, merchants established schools specially for their own needs. Character-building, the social cement, was being wedded to technical skills.[4] It would appear that by the mid-nineteenth century 40 or 50 per cent of boys and 10 to 15 per cent of girls were receiving some form of education.[5]

It was on this secure foundation of social cohesion and practical learning that the Meiji rulers could build, in their efforts to turn Japan into a mighty industrial power and a force to be reckoned with in the modern world. In the early Meiji period a premium was placed on specialist technical knowledge and nearly all trained experts could find gainful employment. Japan could thus avoid the pockets of discontent and pool of unemployed so characteristic of Third World countries since 1945. From the beginning, too, Japanese education was practical, with pupils studying economically relevant subjects, and the system was broadly based, again in contrast with contemporary developing countries. Importantly, a major objective was to acquire and disseminate technical knowhow from abroad, and Japan's success in foreign markets during the years from 1945 to the 1970s rested on an ability to improve upon overseas inventions. As a result, foreign experts employed in Japan were more numerous in the early Meiji period than later.[6]

Consequently, avenues of recruitment and channels of social mobility were being institutionalized – almost as early, in fact, as was the case in Western countries subject to the industrial revolution. For example, while from Meiji times the main state-funded university, Tokyo, supplied many civil servants, the private universities of Keio and Waseda sent their graduates to big business. Another feature of Japanese education has been its dual nature: the system is heavily funded by government but a substantial private sector has been free to experiment and satisfy needs not met by the state.

Education's function as an agent of social mobility grew, producing a meritocracy and new forms of stratification; yet the individual's commitment to the group – exemplified, for instance, by employment patterns based on patron–client relationships between university cliques and industrial corporations – tended to mitigate discontent and provide social mobility in an ever-changing world.

By 1868 the merit principle was being firmly established, and indeed made possible the rise to prominence, after the Meiji Restoration, of sons of low-ranking *Samurai* who had long been excluded from the highest office during the Tokugawa period. But the Meiji oligarchs, drawn mainly from *Samurai* of the southern and western domains, had been educated to leadership in the old secure world of the Tokugawa and thus possessed the confidence and personal stability to carry through the momentous reforms of the new regime.[7]

The goal of Japanese leaders was national integration. The new states of Asia and Africa in contemporary times have faced the problem of creating nations out of ethnic diversity, from tribes divided by the arbitrary boundaries of colonial powers. The task of the Meiji leaders, however, was facilitated because the Japanese people were homogeneous, lacking significant racial minorities; and so successful were policies relating to education, conscription, improvement of communications and the establishment of a bureaucracy that the main process of nation-building, the inculcation of a national consciousness, had been virtually accomplished by the end of the nineteenth century.

To survive in a hostile world and regain Japanese sovereignty in the face of the 'unequal' treaties imposed by foreign powers, the new rulers had to compete with the West on its own terms. This meant the creation of an advanced industrial economy which could be achieved only through social discipline and an efficient national administration. Unity was the watchword, and political dissent could be tolerated only within narrow limits.

Loyalty to the Emperor system by all classes of Japanese, and traditional social values of hierarchy, provided a secure anchorage in a period of transition. The 1890 Constitution set up a national legislature, but the role of the executive remained paramount; autonomous political organization was severely circumscribed, with political parties able to control cabinets only through alliance with factions of the bureaucracy. In addition Imperial advisers, like elder statesmen and senior officers in the armed forces, wielded considerable extra-constitutional power. An authoritarian tradition predisposed constitution-makers to stress the duties, not the rights, of citizens; parliamentary institutions were created merely as a concession to those prominent figures denied the levers of political power after 1868 and as a means of forging national unity. Legislation was an instrument of national policy in the hands of a self-appointed oligarchy. The Japanese experience suggests that there are various ways of achieving a consensus. Many parliamentary institutions were Western but the political process was uniquely Japanese. The populace had no conception of being able to influence government but looked to it for the satisfaction of economic needs and social stability.

But Japan's sense of identity has been less certain. Although the existence of competing domains introduced the idea of rival states, thus enabling them to accept a concept of international relations, the Japanese initially saw their country as holding a rather precarious position between East and West, a Victorian parvenu not yet at home in a European-dominated world order. Only in 1911, fifty-odd years after the first 'unequal' treaties, did Japan succeed in regaining tariff autonomy and in eliminating extraterritoriality, the system by which foreign powers could set up their own courts in Japan to try their own nationals. But Western countries were still unwilling to accord Japan what her citizens believed to be appropriate status in the international order, and such slights strengthened the hand of those military and economic adventurers who demanded Asian regional leadership as a way of enhancing Japan's world interests. This policy was justified by the ideology of pan-Asianism whereby Japan, the most economically advanced Oriental country and thus leader of Asia, had a divine mission to lead nations like China from backwardness to modernity. This vision – combined with successful modernization – inspired colonial conquest, with resulting defeat in war and American occupation of Japan itself.

The 1946 Constitution, imposed on Japan at the behest of the United States, established Anglo-American-style parliamentary institutions, guaranteeing democratic freedoms and the greater accountability of government. But while these bodies – in terms of civil liberties and popular participation – were a considerable advance on pre-war practice, decision-making processes remained consensual rather than majoritarian, reflecting the traditional subordination of the individual to the group. The old authority patterns and social values which had fired economic growth in the pre-war period once again proved resilient. By the 1930s Japan was in any case already a major industrial power, with the war effort stimulating technical advance. Social discipline has enabled post-war Japanese governments to convince their people of the need to move into the manufacture of new commodities. By the 1960s there was a shift from the former reliance on textiles to heavy industrial products; moves to electronics, and latterly computers and robotics, soon followed. This process of adjustment was considerably aided by the acquisition of American patents and licences. There was also improvement on technology originally developed elsewhere, thereby obviating the necessity for heavy expenditure on research and development during the 1950s and 1960s. Significantly, in the early 1980s the Chinese have been pursuing similar policies by importing software or knowledge as opposed to complete industrial plant.

In summary, Japan's current status as the world's second economic power owes much to a stable policy firmly grounded in traditional social values.

In contrast the Chinese, because of their country's size, abundant natural resources and inherited culture, never felt as vulnerable to Western civilization as did the Japanese. This confidence of their rulers, from the Qing dynasty to the Chinese People's Republic, that China is the centre of civilization has been a mixed blessing, often precluding the worst effects of cultural pollution but at the same time preventing concerted effort to address the Western challenge.

From China's first major military defeats in the Opium War in the mid-nineteenth century, Imperial rulers realized the necessity of strengthening their country's defence but failed to anticipate the changes in political institutions and personal values such policies would ultimately necessitate.

In the last century the real rulers of China were the scholar-officials, or bureaucrats, recruited through a series of competitive examinations based on Confucian classical texts. The bureaucracy was in theory a meritocracy, as Confucianism was egalitarian in its assumption that all men could become rulers by imbibing certain moral principles; but in practice, officialdom became the preserve of gentry families and a charmed circle; the wealthy, the pool from which candidates were drawn, had the means to finance the prolonged study required.

If the scholar-official stood at the top of the status system the merchant was placed on the lowest rung, and all legitimate avenues to power were political. There were government monopolies of important commodities and, as a low premium was placed on entrepreneurial skills, few centres of independent economic power existed. Moreover, the successful merchant, to gain respectability, bought official status; even more significantly he put his wealth into land and, like the peasantry, did not invest in industry, in contrast with nineteenth-century Japanese practice. Consequently, the individualist economic instinct was lacking in China, and European-style capitalism did not develop before the Western impact of the nineteenth century. It is not surprising that, in a culture where political rather than economic relations were paramount, the Chinese should by 1949 have been predisposed to adopt a form of Marxist-Leninist collectivism, as an ideology to turn China into an advanced industrial society and promote her self-appointed role as leader of world revolution.

But although the Chinese still identify their country as the centre of civilization, the creation of viable authority patterns has so far proved a much more formidable task.

It has been said that a despotism is at its most vulnerable the moment it begins to reform itself, and this could be an apt comment on current moves to change the Chinese economic system. Before discussing recent structural changes, however, an evaluation of China's economy as it has operated in modern times is in order. As suggested above, traditionally China did not think highly of the entrepreneur, and capitalism in the Western sense did not develop. At the Communist accession in 1949 the country was still heavily dependent on subsistence agriculture, and most major industries had flourished in the originally foreign-controlled treaty port enclaves, and especially the former Japanese sphere of influence in the Northeast.

Whereas previous Chinese governments had been principally concerned with administration and maintenance of the social *status quo*, the CCP was dedicated to economic growth and political change. Although Marx had envisaged that revolution would take place in the richer industrialized countries of Western Europe the new rulers of China, like their counterparts elsewhere in the Third World, adopted a Marxist-Leninist political system as a means of creating an advanced industrial society.

It was thus with this aim in view that the CCP instituted the Soviet model of central planning, a command economy, whereby the state maintained control of production and consumption, as well as revenue and expenditure at both national and local levels. This did not mean a sharp break with the past, as the previous government, Chiang Kai-shek's Guomindang, following an anti-capitalist ethos, was already in control of main economic sectors and public utilities and feared the challenge which any new independent entrepreneurial wealth might present to the established order. The CCP leaders thus extended state control, gradually transforming private enterprise, and the command economy, as established in the 1950s, remained intact until the late 1970s.

After the death of Mao Zedong in 1976 the new leadership, soon dominated by China's elder statesman, Deng Xiaoping, decided that her ambitious modernization programme could succeed only through increasing foreign trade and economic co-operation with Western powers. Previously, Chinese manufacturers had enjoyed a captive market where consumer choice was strictly limited, but exposure to the rigours of competition abroad and the influx of superior foreign goods have only served to underline the poor quality of Chinese products.

At the root of the problem was the structure of the Chinese economic system; the state allocated raw materials, operating funds and labour, while receiving in return the profits from goods produced, as taxation. Products were subject to state distribution. This proved inefficient and wasteful of resources, stifling any initiative either management or workers may have had, because, as a general rule, after having met relatively low production targets, they were paid regardless of output and quality. Economic reform in the late 1970s and early 1980s has thus been designed to provide much-needed incentive for the workforce and make management more responsive to market forces and consumer demand.

Any concessions by the current leadership to market forces and the profit motive do not, however, mean that the command economy has been abandoned. Most major Chinese industries are still led and financed by the state or are subject to the joint jurisdiction of central and local governments. Recent measures have been designed to render China's economy more efficient and ensure better use of available financial resources. Formerly, for example, capital investment in industry took the form of state appropriations; now the state bank provides loans, in the hope that recipient enterprises will practise stricter cost accounting and achieve maximum economic results. Similarly, funds for innovation and facility improvement, in the past furnished free of charge from the treasury, are now lent by the People's Construction Bank of China.[8] Under this new economic responsibility system enterprises are still subject to tax but are now given greater initiative, and as a reward for efficient management are now allowed to retain profits for investment and may allocate bonuses to workers.[9]

The quality of the labour force is also a crucial determinant of economic success. Until the late 1970s manpower was distributed by the state and had a meal ticket for life; enterprises may now hire and fire workers, who also have a new freedom to change jobs.[10] Thus labour performance may be more closely monitored to allow for manpower selection on merit, the idea being to encourage innovative skills on both sides of industry. In addition, to prevent duplication of effort and promote greater variety of products, economic planners are taking steps to facilitate greater co-ordination and co-operation within industries.[11] Finally, contracts are now signed between manufacturers and buyers so that goods comply with customers' designs and specifications.[12]

Nevertheless, in a command economy like China's a balance must be struck between the revenue needs of the state and incentives for industries and localities; as of 1983 increases in profits retained by enterprises have resulted in a decline in the funds accumulated for the national treasury.[13]

It is, however, far easier to reform institutions than change values and attitudes that determine the way in which an economic system is actually operated. Deng Xiaoping and his supporters have staked their own reputations and, by extension, the CCP's credibility on economic performance, but the implementation of their policies is to some extent still being impeded by leftist elements who came to prominence in the Cultural Revolution (1966–9), a movement launched by Mao Zedong to destroy his political opponents and prevent the re-emergence of the kind of privilege which he believed existed in pre-1949 China. The remnants of this group, formerly led by Jiang Qing, have much to lose from what they see as a reversal of the late Chairman's position. The leftist stance has been fundamentally anti-intellectual, stressing 'redness' or political acceptability rather than the reward of experts in the service of the modernization programme; the former view implicitly rejects economic co-operation with the West.

Because of such factors as the abolition of primogeniture and the propensity of successful entrepreneurs to invest in land Chinese family-type loyalties, unlike those in Japan, have not always proved conducive to economic growth, and the Cultural Revolution, by fomenting struggle between revolutionaries and power-holders (especially in industry) has bequeathed to China a legacy of factionalism, thereby only confirming traditional-type loyalties. The majority, caught in the crossfire of conflict, turned for support to their own personal connections, friends and family, the only people whom they could implicitly trust.

These trends have bred caution: factory middle management, for instance, has been reticent about carrying out such policies as material incentives and promotion on merit lest these be subsequently reversed on a change of national leadership. Leftists, who came to power under the aegis of the Gang of Four, see their vested interests threatened by the new emphasis on technical expertise. The old Chinese view that all relationships are political and that with power goes wealth is reinforced: state control of the command economy has inherited the habits of the Imperial bureaucracy.

The greater freedom granted to enterprises was designed to enhance technical expertise, promote innovation, provide worker incentives and guarantee better-quality goods. But CCP members still control factory operations and are reluctant to listen to the views of technical personnel, who consequently cannot realize their full potential and put to work the managerial training many of them have acquired overseas. Incentives are seen as the key to economic success but old practices like the 'iron rice-bowl' – or permanent tenure of employment – low wage differentials, as well as arguments over criteria for determining worthy recipients, have resulted in the distribution of bonuses all round as a kind of wage increase. Congresses of workers and staff have been established to air the views of all, but many are still reluctant to challenge Party secretaries who are responsible not to the workforce as a whole but to their superiors in the CCP hierarchy. The power to dismiss, originally intended to eliminate the incompetent, is so often being used as a weapon by the dominant faction in an enterprise against those outside their group.[14]

The traditional social system could thus in the long term prove a mixed blessing for the Chinese economy. The new emphasis on family farming, instead of the earlier system of collective agriculture under more direct state control, has undoubtedly led to increases in productivity but heads of household have seen the labour of all as so vital that children are now frequently kept from school, and this could eventually result in the lowering of educational standards to the ultimate detriment of economic development as a whole. The further growth of agriculture will in any case depend on massive state finance in such areas as irrigation improvement and mechanization; future advance will require a balance of public and private initiatives.

Thus the events of the Cultural Revolution and the recent reassessment of Mao Zedong's contribution to the Chinese revolution have severely dented the CCP's credibility, and both political stability and economic growth will clearly depend on the current leadership's ability to restore the Party's legitimacy in the eyes of the Chinese people. Education will play a crucial role in this process, its function being twofold: the training of experts and the inculcation of political loyalty in coming generations. Already instruction in Communist principles has been reintroduced in the education system, particularly in primary schools, and the absorption of foreign technology, for instance, will always require moral as well as purely technical choices.

The current leadership have exalted the position of the intellectual – defined as anyone with secondary education or above – in contemporary China, thus reversing the stance of Mao Zedong who, while never rejecting the need for experts, saw them essentially as potential critics of the society in which they lived. In his view Communist egalitarian social goals were even more vital than the demands of a developing economy; to make intellectuals – as in traditional China – servants of a ruling orthodoxy rather than independent professionals, he insisted that they be remoulded through participation in manual labour in the rural areas and strove to create a class of mental labourers drawn from ordinary workers and peasants and thus responsive to the CCP's will.

In contrast, intellectuals will now be judged by their contribution to China's modernization programme and any manual labour required will be directly related to study, for example, of agricultural experimental plots, with trips made to the countryside intended to impart professional knowledge to local peasants.

For much of the Cultural Revolution period, universities and secondary schools were closed while students were encouraged to campaign against Mao's opponents in the leadership; consequently, a whole generation was deprived of university study and there has since been a shortage of qualified manpower.

In an attempt to catch up with the advanced academic levels of the Western world, students have been sent abroad in larger numbers than ever before and Chinese universities have undertaken faculty exchanges with Western countries. Scientific research projects, before the late 1970s undertaken almost exclusively in the institutes of the Academy of Sciences, are now being pursued in the universities, and both types of institution will now be staffed by foreign-trained Chinese graduates even though ultimately, of course, this manpower must come from China's own education system. There is a determination, too, to apply the fruits of scientific research more directly and aptly to industrial production, thereby making better use of scarce resources.

That Chinese intellectuals are in short supply, especially considering the major task before them, is indicated by the following statistics. According to a recent Chinese census, in 1983 intellectuals of university standard represented only 0.9 per cent of the country's population over the age of twenty-five; this compares unfavourably with an equivalent figure for Japan of 14.4 per cent in 1980 and one of 31.1 per cent for the United States in 1979, with a similarly computed ratio for those over twenty years old in the Soviet Union being 7.2 per cent in 1970.[15]

China's leaders believe that the 1983 total of 1.35 million full-time university and college students, a smaller proportion of the population than in the developed countries, is inadequate for China's future economic needs and funds spent on education as a whole are being accordingly increased, with 15.9 per cent of state expenditure devoted to that sector, including health and culture – a 4.9 per cent increase over the previous plan.[16]

There are now 715 full-time institutions of higher education as opposed to 598 in 1978, and it is projected that numbers in such institutions will reach 1.76 million by 1987.[17] Postgraduate education will also be further developed, total enrolment being expected to reach 20,000 in 1985 compared to the 11,000 studying in 1981.

However, because expansion of full-time higher education cannot keep pace with national needs and popular demand, localities and enterprises are establishing, mainly out of their own funds, various kinds of part-time study institutions catering for adults whose schooling was interrupted by the Cultural Revolution as well as those secondary school graduates who fail the highly competitive full-time university enrolment examination. These bodies, usually receiving no outlay from the state treasury, have a further cost advantage.

While it takes 8000 to 10,000 Chinese dollars to train a four-year full-time university student, a local university in the city of Shenyang was said to spend only 1000 dollars on a student taking a two-year course.[18] In addition, full use is being made of educational television and radio together with correspondence courses. Finally, although full-time higher education is generally residential, providing scholarships or financial aid, day students are now being enrolled and funded by enterprises from profits or by fee-paying parents.[19]

But China urgently needs not just high-powered technologists but middle-level technical personnel to staff her increasingly complex bureaucracy, industrial establishment, and growing numbers of private commercial enterprises. Given that only a small percentage of graduates will be able to enter higher education, the secondary system is being more broadly structured, perhaps with the Japanese model in mind. More vocational institutions are being established and technical subjects added to curricula, even in the more academically oriented schools.

Acceleration of technological change surely means that China cannot allow ability to be wasted, and every effort is being made to tap talent from all sources. Stress on academic excellence may well be fostering a meritocracy, even if equality of opportunity is yet to be achieved. The competitive nature of university enrolment examinations has already been noted, and in 1983 only one in five candidates was being accepted for entry.[20] The net, however, is being cast widely to attract those with practical experience and potential for advanced study; young workers up to the age of twenty-eight who score at least 80 per cent of the pass mark and show further promise are being offered special concessions, like preparatory classes, to enable them later to join regular courses in universities.[21]

Moreover, although the alumni of prestigious full-time institutions will no doubt for some time to come be better placed to gain lucrative employment, all graduates – officially at least – regardless of educational background and social origin, will be granted equal opportunity and status in employment.

Social mobility does not preclude social stratification and

China's present education system is élitist as well as merito-cratic. There are now two systems of education, and within the full-time sector some institutions, in both the humanities and the sciences, are being designated 'key point' and receive a disproportionate amount of state funding. Consequently, they can select the most qualified among the large number of applicants they attract. On application for higher education candidates may select subject preferences, but their choice has in the past not necessarily coincided with the nation's priori-ties. In the final months before the university enrolment examinations great attention is paid to the political education of candidates, the task being to convince them to opt for those less popular and less prestigious, though still naturally impor-tant, fields like pedagogy, agriculture, forestry, geology and mining.[22] Traditionally, moreover, education was always held in high esteem as the road to official position; some parents are now criticized for encouraging candidates to study in famous city universities because this will bring the family honour and fortune. In contrast, true moral quality is said to lie in eagerness to serve the national interest.

China's economic survival depends on the absorption of foreign technology and its adaptation to Chinese conditions, but this process will always require moral, in addition to purely technical, choices. Accordingly, the heavy emphasis on scientific subjects in universities during the late 1970s has now been modified; the liberal arts and humanities have their part to play in equipping future generalist administrators and industrial management to take a broad view of wider issues in the light of CCP doctrine.

The Chinese leaders have implicitly acknowledged that in the contemporary world a nation's wealth lies in realizing the full potential of outstanding individuals. China's intellectuals, through travel abroad and study at home, are being more than ever exposed to foreign institutions, ideas and tastes. But this increased exposure to Western material culture and technology is inevitably leading to new social tensions and problems of political control. At present China's intelligentsia are being given greater freedom of expression than that granted to the population at large, because of their unique scientific and technological contribution to economic development, but the CCP leaders are already taking steps to define the boundaries of intellectual and artistic dissent. Moreover, there is always the danger that Chinese students abroad may defect and secure a standard of living higher than that available at home.

As the frontiers of knowledge advance so do even the tasks of ordinary workers, especially in industry, grow more complex; and social controls must become more sophisticated, particularly in a totalitarian setting like China.

China's rulers are slowly beginning to accept that leadership in industry is not simply a matter of exhortation by cadres; application of new technology and a more efficient workforce are possible only through modern professional management techniques. In fact, as a result of poor management, some newly imported equipment is operating below capacity.

Thus cadres are now being enrolled in enterprise management courses at universities, and the Chinese Association of Enterprise Management has been charged with the task of studying foreign systems.[23] With the possible exception of Shanghai, Chinese standards of management and business accounting systems are way below those overseas, and it is in these fields that the Chinese have sought co-operation with Japan, concluding that the secrets of Japanese economic success have lain in improving productivity. Although Japan's experience cannot be duplicated elsewhere certain lessons may be learned, and a government body, the Japan International Co-operation Agency, has been entrusted with the training of selected Chinese managers, who carry out reform of management methods on their return to China. In addition, China's Association of Enterprise Management is building a training centre in Tianjin with Japanese government aid.[24]

If better management techniques are being fostered to create a more predictable environment for industrial progress, by the same token the greater economic initiative granted to localities and enterprises, together with increased foreign trade and co-operation, demand a more comprehensive and precise legal framework.

Although at pains to assure foreign partners of China's

political stability and a fair return on their investments, China's leaders have admitted deficiencies in their country's legal system. In 1979 the Chinese examined a collection of foreign investment laws from developing countries, compiled by Japanese trading companies, before preparing China's law on joint ventures. Foreign banking expertise is similarly being examined.

In conclusion, recent economic reforms have been designed to unleash the energies of outstanding individuals who will be personally rewarded for their contribution to China's modernization programme. The absorption of foreign technology and the country's need to compete successfully on world markets demand a highly qualified labour force at all levels; education – increasingly élitist and meritocratic – will become, as in Japan and other major industrial states, the main channel of social mobility.

Increasing provision of primary and secondary education is in turn creating further demand for university study and this, in conjunction with exposure to Western culture through the mass media and Western contacts, is creating rising expectations, a potential source of social discord. Growing income disparity seems an almost inevitable concomitant of economic development in Third World countries; in China the real division is between the cities, endowed with better amenities overall – especially in relation to education and health – and the countryside, in general disadvantaged. In addition, there are signs of regional differentiation in wealth; the household contract system, whereby farming families, providing they fulfil state quotas, have greater freedom in planting and selling crops, brings income variation even within the same production team, and workers in rural industries are often paid more than those performing purely agricultural tasks.

Only the legitimacy and credibility of the CCP as representative of the wider national interest can ensure the kind of social discipline crucial for long-term political stability and economic success. Meanwhile the Japanese are helping China's rulers to create the preconditions, the philosophical infrastructure, on which future trade and economic co-operation between the two countries may be built.

3 China's Economic Strategy: The relevance of Japan's experience

The prerequisites of modernization, a term which has come to be associated with the advanced industrial economies of present-day Western countries, are those values and attitudes conducive to the creation of native, or the utilization of foreign, technology. In underdeveloped countries, for example those of the contemporary Third World in Asia, Africa and Latin America, the wealth indispensable for advanced economic development can be derived from one or both of two main sources: the indigenous primary sector or investment in technology from abroad. Japan has often been referred to as one of the few examples of successful modernization in the non-Western world and, although its achievement was undoubtedly due to certain traditional social factors, a common cultural heritage is shared with China. Tracing development in the two countries before the end of the Second World War will provide a comparative perspective against which current Chinese economic strategy may be viewed.

Wishing to avoid the fate that had befallen the Chinese Empire, the Meiji oligarchs dedicated themselves to the task of creating a strong Japan better able to resist the infringement of sovereignty by colonial powers. In the nineteenth century subsistence agriculture remained the basis of the Japanese economy; modernization was possible only through exploitation of the primary sector and the introduction of foreign technology, the basis of the West's armed superiority. But technological change can be brought about only in a favourable political and economic environment.

Certain traditional features of the Japanese economic system were conducive to such policies of development, as was the achievement of national unity in 1868. The new rulers built on foundations already laid by the old domain governments; land taxes had already been high and the Meiji leaders increased them. It has been estimated that the primary sector accounted for about two-thirds of the national income until 1882, and it was clear that growth in the secondary and tertiary sectors would be financed mainly by exploiting agriculture. By the early 1880s no less than 78 per cent of the government's revenues were being derived from the land tax. Although the peasantry were initially disadvantaged as the bulk of the revenues were channelled into the creation of a modern communications system, the industrialization programme and the furtherance of national defence, agriculture and the rural areas were not neglected; for good social as well as economic reasons finance was devoted to increasing agricultural yields through experimental stations and technical education. Social cohesion was maintained by increases in agricultural production without initially implementing changes in the land tenure system. Simultaneously, the land tax was an integrating force, as peasants became more aware of their role in the national economy.[1]

These policies of national integration were crucial if Japan were to maintain her independence and achieve world-power status. Thus while technology and experts were imported from abroad, capital for development was generated from within Japan and until the early years of the twentieth century the traditional sector remained vital to the creation of a modern economy. As such physical infrastructure as railways and communications were laid and textile industries as well as metallurgy furthered through domestic savings, Japan emerged by the early 1930s as a semi-developed country, possessing a light and semi-heavy industrial base. It was not until after the First World War that the development of various branches of heavy industry demanded the input of foreign investment.[2]

Meanwhile, international events were proving a stimulus to technical innovation. In reaction to the world depression of the late 1920s, increasing diplomatic isolation, and forces seen as beyond the nation's control, Japan's establishment was being pressured by extremist forces at home towards further territorial expansion on the Asian mainland. War preparations stimulated effort in the machine-building sector which ultimately created skills and technological 'spin-off' later applied to civilian manufacturing, thereby laying the basis for innovation in post-war Japan.[3] Then as now Japanese success has depended very largely on the improvement of imported technology, a process which itself produced human skills applicable to other sectors.

The events of the Cold War were favourable to Japan's economic growth as United States Occupation policies shifted from demilitarization of an erstwhile enemy to rehabilitation of a new ally in the struggle against Communism in Asia. Initially, Japanese recovery benefited from American procurement contracts for the Korean War effort and introduction to world markets by the United States.

Japan's ability to compete in these new markets was facilitated by a highly educated workforce, adequate labour supplies and a continuing process of capital accumulation. During the 1950s and 1960s the centre of gravity in the Japanese economy shifted from light to heavy industry, with the latter enjoying the bulk of investment by the private sector and a significant proportion of technical innovation.[4] But such a transition would not have been possible without the purchase of foreign patents, about three-quarters of which were American, for use in the machinery, electrical goods, and chemical industries.[5] Improving on this technology in the 1970s and 1980s, the Japanese have acquired a competitive edge – often by virtue of better design and efficiency – in markets for television sets and computers.

If a highly disciplined adaptable population made improvement of imported technology both possible and profitable, investment from abroad, although considerable in absolute terms, played a less significant role, as it represented only about 2 per cent of the domestic funds made available to Japanese industry.[6] Because of their ability to learn from United States capitalism, the Japanese have been considered champions of private enterprise. Yet, while most capital accumulation has been derived from the private sector, government investment has nevertheless been considerable. In many countries the state controls major public utilities, but Japanese governments have played a greater role in capital investment than would have been expected in a society so dedicated to the principles of a free market economy. In such areas as infrastructure and land improvement the volume of government activity has been similar to that of developing countries. In addition high levels of personal savings, deposited in government banks and savings accounts, have enabled successive Japanese governments to lend funds for investment in key industries and export financing.[7]

Thus a crucial factor in Japan's economic success during the last century has been the social cohesion contributed by the relationship between Japanese government and business. Such apparent unity of purpose, often remarked upon in the context of post-1945 Japan, was nevertheless originally inspired by the commonly perceived threat of foreign encroachment, and the Meiji leaders were able to build on a long tradition of domain intervention in economic affairs. Tokugawa society's clearly defined status system restricted both occupational mobility and consumption patterns but, as this structure began to break down in the wake of the socio-economic changes occasioned by two hundred years of internal peace under Bakufu rule, economic controls began to shift to markets, prices and production. Not only did the Shogunate directly administer the major financial and commodity markets of Osaka, it controlled major natural resources like mines and forests. Additionally, and more significantly, any new economic enterprise needed government approval. Similar economic controls were imposed by the domains and increased with greater independence from a weakened Bakufu in the face of foreign demands for treaties. The domains became states within a state and their governments placed some important products under the jurisdiction of official marketing boards from production to purchase. A number of these boards evolved into private companies after national unification during the Meiji period. This legacy, familiar to the leaders who gained power nationally after 1868, together with the commutation of *Samurai* stipends for later investment in industrial enterprises, forged the link between Meiji government and business, a heritage which has come to be seen as a key factor in Japan's post-war economic miracle.[8]

China, like Japan, was still an economically under-developed country in the mid-nineteenth century but her response to the West was less effective, as unequal treaties limited sovereignty, permitted the creation of spheres of influence, and facilitated economic penetration by colonial powers. As a result of foreign pressure central control over the provinces weakened, resulting in traditional peasant rebellion and modern revolutionary movements, and the colonial enclaves on the coast became safe havens where modern industry could develop under the auspices of foreign entrepreneurs in collaboration with Chinese compradors. In addition, however, even if China lacked the national unity and social cohesion of Japan, Chinese Imperial officials similarly realized the need for modernization, and it was through the efforts of increasingly powerful regional figures to enhance military potential that modern techniques were introduced for the development of arsenals, factories, and transport facilities.[9] This establishment of infrastructure and communications had two main implications for the Chinese economy: a demand was created for repairs and ancillary services and newly recruited Chinese apprentices could learn their trade from skilled foreign mechanics. Chinese ancillary industries then developed to service modern transport and communications, and this experience subsequently made possible native production of such goods as railway equipment and small ships.

But there were limits to the expansion of industrial potential through repair services, and serious constraints on Chinese economic development during the pre-1949 period. The iron and steel industry, for example, could be developed only by considerable injection of capital from overseas and the reinvestment of profits which, in contrast to Japanese experience, meant foreign control.[10] Furthermore, the fact that much foreign trade and direct investment was confined to the treaty ports restricted their contribution to the Chinese domestic economy as a whole. Finally, political disunity and lack of central Chinese government control over the country's economic destiny tended to inhibit capital accumulation for development.

The appeal of the CCP leaders to the populace had lain in their creation of an integrative ideology through the adaptation of Marxism-Leninism to Chinese conditions; they thereby satisfied the two demands of nationalism and modernization. In 1949 they brought a semblance of national unity and stability, promising to turn China into an advanced industrial society. Although, in retrospect, the Sino–Soviet Treaty of Friendship in 1950 proved a marriage of temporary convenience rather than a permanent alliance, it brought to China the tangible gains of economic and technical assistance, albeit in the form of loans as opposed to outright aid. The Soviet connection and the gradual creation of a command economy through initial restriction and ultimate elimination of private enterprise made possible capital generation on a national scale. Moreover, the Chinese could build on the technical foundation of the pre-war period and release energies held back by decades of civil strife, foreign economic penetration and resulting capital scarcity. Thus during the period of China's Soviet-inspired First Five-year Plan (1953–7), the enormous growth in heavy industrial resources and output was stimulated both by pre-war untapped technical potential and the technological input provided by Soviet equipment and advisers. The cycle was then repeated as these new inputs promoted ancillary services and skills, later to be applied to other areas of production.[11]

Thus industry advanced on two fronts: the establishment of enterprises with up-to-date Soviet equipment, for example in Manchuria, and the evolution of factories like the Shanghai Machine Tools Plant, which had developed from an old agricultural machine shop.[12] Although the two approaches have never been mutually exclusive but a matter of relative emphasis, the withdrawal of Russian technicians and blueprints in 1960 at the beginning of the Sino–Soviet dispute led Mao Zedong to make a virtue out of necessity and stress policies of national self-reliance.

Soviet-style central planning had given priority to heavy

industry at the expense of agriculture, which was expected to provide raw materials for light industry at home; the latter in turn was charged with the task of producing exports to be exchanged for capital goods from abroad, notably the Soviet Union and Eastern Europe, until China's pattern of world trade changed in the mid-1960s. Slow increases in agricultural yields, however, continued to retard growth in other economic sectors, and the policies of decentralization and regional self-sufficiency instituted in the Great Leap Forward, beginning in 1958, were designed to improve agricultural efficiency through locally generated capital and technical improvisation.

Although central government assistance was never precluded, it was intended that locally run agricultural service industries and fertilizer plants, for instance, would produce the skills and experience necessary for the achievement of higher agricultural yields as well as the industrialization of the rural areas.

By the early 1970s the Chinese leaders' perception of encirclement by the Soviet Union as well as the United States was forcing a reassessment of China's foreign relations. Furthermore there were clearly limits to policies of economic self-help, and increasingly the importation of Western technology was seen as crucial to China's recently formulated modernization programme. But the Gang of Four, led by Jiang Qing, did not support this new stance on foreign trade and sought to champion national self-sufficiency both as a desirable quality in itself and as a weapon directed against the rest of the CCP leadership in the struggle to succeed the ageing Mao, in whose name they claimed to speak.

After the Gang's political defeat at the hands of Mao's successor Hua Guofeng, their policies were attacked as wasteful of manpower and material resources because of duplication of effort on problems already solved by more advanced countries. China's chemical fibre industry was cited as a positive example where improved technology had helped to raise levels of quality and production. Technology in the manufacture of vinylon had been imported in the early 1960s, and a decade later similar equipment was being manufactured in China itself.[13]

In contrast to the radicals' self-sufficiency approach, Mao's policy of self-reliance had stressed the critical study of foreign equipment and the need to improve upon it, and in this respect it came close to Japanese practice. In fact, in October 1978 an article in the *Beijing Review* referred to Japan's acquisition of patent rights as an ideal method of absorbing technology and then modifying it to suit native conditions.[14]

The introduction of foreign – mainly Western – capital, technology and equipment, approved by Mao Zedong and Premier Zhou Enlai in the early 1970s, was now regarded as a long-term strategic policy decision and the only solution for primitive production techniques and low labour productivity.

The last years of Mao Zedong's life nevertheless saw a succession struggle between moderate and radical factions within the Chinese leadership together with conflicting approaches to development strategy, bringing into focus pace and method of technology input from abroad. To bridge the gap between competing factions, Mao Zedong nominated a hitherto little-known agricultural expert with impeccable revolutionary credentials, Hua Guofeng, as his successor. With the aid of the moderates associated with the then still disgraced Deng Xiaoping and certain military leaders, Hua moved rapidly to eliminate politically the radical Gang of Four, and in 1977 and 1978 began to unveil the Four Modernizations – agriculture, industry, national defence, and science and technology – a more ambitious version of the programme outlined by Zhou Enlai in the early seventies.

Mao Zedong, in common with the leaders of other developing countries, was dedicated to the creation of an advanced industrial society; but his priorities differed in that he had a greater concern for egalitarian social goals than for the demands of a developing economy. He saw distribution of wealth as more important than its accumulation. Accordingly, political commitment to the creation of a new society assumed greater importance than the training of a technocratic élite. This personal quality was summed up in the phrase 'red and expert', but the value of the former component outweighed that of the latter. The two priorities of 'red and expert' are not mutually exclusive, however, and balancing them is a matter of emphasis. This is a continuing dilemma for the CCP and, in spite of the post-Mao leadership's stress on technical expertise, a man's character or political quality is considered at least as important as his professional competence.

Hua, in order better to utilize professional qualifications *per se*, enhanced the privileges enjoyed by experts, although his economic programme retained many of the features of Maoist planning. While the history of the industrial revolution in Europe demonstrated that economic growth is rarely regionally even, as advantages so often accrue to human and material resource-rich areas, CCP policy had opted until the late 1970s for balanced development throughout the country; in China the state controlled key economic sectors like heavy industry and decentralized planning involved commitment to local self-sufficiency, especially in food.

According to this policy of balanced development and equal distribution, steel manufacture – the basis of heavy industry – and grain production – crucial to feed a growing population and obviate the necessity of spending precious foreign exchange on food imports – were seen as keys to economic success.

Within the framework of central government planning from the 1950s onwards, regional authorities were therefore encouraged to vie with one another in building heavy industries, with resulting duplication of effort among many medium and small enterprises and little regard to such factors as local resources and transport facilities. Consequently there was considerable wastage, quality control suffered, and unprofitable operations placed a heavy burden on local finance.

It would have made more sense to concentrate the limited capital and resources available on industrial development in the more advanced coastal regions, which in any case achieved substantial growth and were accounting for as much as two-thirds of total national industrial output even as late as the early 1980s. Nevertheless, many of the formerly least industrialized interior regions of China – like Gansu and Inner Mongolia – produced the country's highest rates of industrial growth. The CCP placed a premium on opening up and developing the inland regions; as a result, the creation of infrastructure in the form of railway and electric power projects in the hinterland meant bottlenecks in the same sectors on the coast.[15]

If planning of heavy industry and infrastructure had its defects, agricultural policy was, in retrospect, equally suspect. Before the late 1970s the policy of making grain the key link held sway; that is, the Maoist view gave priority to the attainment of local self-sufficiency in food and accumulating grain reserves everywhere, thereby placing constraints on specialization in cash crops.

At the First Session of the Fifth National People's Congress in 1978 Hua Guofeng reaffirmed these principles and set what later proved to be over-ambitious targets for grain and steel. Hua's economic strategy thus resembled the Maoist approach in its stress on heavy industry but his programme as a whole differed from earlier practice in scale, ambition and its greater emphasis on the role of technical experts, import of technology from abroad and tentative steps towards acceptance of foreign investment.

The domestic targets, however, soon proved unrealistic. The CCP leaders were in any case operating in an unfamiliar terrain. China's percentage of world trade was still small, but now production and provision of exports in exchange for technology imports were subjecting the economy to market forces beyond the leadership's control. In addition, credits from abroad also had to be repaid. Sizeable trade deficits were being incurred, reviving fears of indebtedness and foreign economic domination, especially in view of earlier experience with the Soviet Union. Quality control was now increasingly necessary to make China's goods competitive.

Hua Guofeng and his supporters were providing material incentives for workers as well as scientists and technologists but this did not alter the structure of the Chinese command economy, which had been built to eschew the profit motive. Consequently, the system was not proving amenable to the new demands being placed upon it. Economic reverses, together with a new political balance of power within China's ruling circles, combined to discredit Hua Guofeng's leadership. As a second-generation leader, brought rapidly to the fore by Mao, Hua lacked the ties of a powerful clique, like that headed by Deng Xiaoping.

The gradual rehabilitation in July 1977 of moderate elements – including Deng – who had been purged in the Cultural Revolution gradually began to undermine Hua's precarious position. Throughout 1978 'rebel' economists, some of whom had opposed Mao's policies in the Great Leap Forward and had subsequently been responsible for economic recovery in the early 1960s, were being reinstated under Deng Xiaoping's auspices and undertook a re-evaluation of the 'Four Modernizations' programme. They started to challenge the system of Soviet-type central planning instituted during the 1950s, and at the Third Plenum of the Eleventh Central Committee in 1978 there was a call for readjustment in economic policy involving greater attention to the profit motive and market forces. From henceforth economic levers rather than administrative planning would manage the economy.[16]

The case for a form of market socialism, implied in the measures adopted by economists like Chen Yun in the early 1960s but halted by the Cultural Revolution, were enshrined in the economic readjustment policy outlined at the Second Session of the Fifth National People's Congress by Vice-Premier Yu Qiuli in his report on the national economic plan for 1979.

Readjustment was a watershed in post-1949 China because it reflected the leadership's implicit recognition that thirty years of Communist rule had stifled personal initiative and innovation, and that the energies of the population could be released only with promises of a better life and provision of material well-being. Ideological incentives and political controls have not been abandoned but there is, at least, a belated acknowledgement that social and economic inequality among individuals and between regions, for example, will be a fact of life for some decades to come. China's natural resources are boundless, but her ultimate wealth lies in the genius of her people in exploiting those resources through native expertise developed in collaboration with foreign technology.

Thus Deng Xiaoping and his supporters, by 1979 replacing

the Hua Guofeng leadership as key decision-makers, concluded that previous policies of equal distribution, balanced development and emphasis on developing the inland regions had created tensions and disequilibrium in the Chinese economy. They sought to effect readjustment on the basis of principles recognizing market forces and the profit motive, while retaining certain aspects of Soviet-type central planning characteristic of a Marxist-Leninist political system. This reform programme was scheduled to cover the period of the Sixth Five-year Plan (1981–5) and possibly beyond, and designed to produce faster economic growth through material incentives at home in addition to export competitiveness abroad.

The keynotes were flexible planning and better use of existing resources. In 1982 Premier Zhao Ziyang noted the rigidity of past Five-year Plans; such plans are in future sure to play a guiding and supporting role, with emphasis on better long-term planning by commissions, ministries and provincial authorities, with adjustments made according to changing circumstances and local conditions. There is, however, still the long-term official target of quadrupling industrial and agricultural output by the year 2000, implying an ambitious annual growth of 7.2 per cent in real terms over the rest of the century.[17] According to Zhao, the heavy budget deficits of the late 1970s and early 1980s are to be eliminated and economic recovery achieved through strict control of government expenditure and money supply. Industry is being streamlined to raise productivity and reduce inefficiency in the hope that China's exports may be increasingly attractive to foreign buyers and trade deficits decreased, even in the face of world recession.

Thus Chinese economic planners have been compelled to formulate readjustment policies with international economic trends in view. In his aforementioned speech to the Second Session of the Fifth National People's Congress, outlining the 1979 National Economic Plan, Vice-Premier Yu Quili listed four priorities: (1) emphasis on strengthening China's weak link, infrastructure, together with energy resource development and conservation; (2) the improvement of agricultural production; (3) the promotion of light industry with concomitant reduction of investment in capital construction, especially in relation to heavy industry, and (4) the furtherance of foreign trade, particularly export growth, and the utilization of foreign technology. After consideration of these priorities, the performance of the respective economic sectors since the initiation of readjustment will be evaluated.

Better communications and transport facilities are the key to political and economic integration, the *sine qua non* of an advanced industrial society, and these sectors, together with energy, are being allotted 39 per cent of total investment in the Sixth Five-year Plan.[18] But although postal and other links are to be increased, stress until 1985 will be on expanding existing communication lines rather than constructing new systems. In a country where, traditionally, vast areas had few transport facilities railways, roads and waterways are being given investment priority. It is projected, for example, that rail-passenger-carrying capacity will increase annually by 6 per cent during the coming years, with rail-freight volume at least doubling by the year 2000. Paved highways will also be doubled in length by 1990.[19] Public facilities and amenities within cities are to be improved.

China's energy supplies are crucial to its future economic development. In the early 1970s, for instance, in their enthusiasm to sell natural resources like petroleum to such countries as Japan in exchange for technology, Chinese economic planners overestimated the immediate potential of local oil production, with the resulting cancellation of the Baoshan steel complex project in Shanghai, for example, in the late 1970s.

In any case, with continuing economic growth, China's own domestic energy needs will increase. Existing industrial facilities have often been working below capacity because of energy shortages. Energy conservation is thus seen as crucial to the success of the modernization programme; large energy-consuming projects are to be delayed for the time being. According to the New China News Agency, the US$6000 million spent on conservation between 1979 and 1982 had saved 19 million tons of coal and 8 million tons of oil.

Nevertheless, although output of coal, which supplies 70 per cent of China's energy, was 4.5 per cent higher in 1982 than in 1971 it was still insufficient to keep pace with industry's demands. While foreign investment is being invited for prospecting and exploitation of both onshore and offshore oilfields, with an eye to the long-term export market, in China itself it is general government policy to burn coal instead of oil.[20] Coal production is being stepped up through the technical transformation of existing mines, with new fields being brought into operation when quick returns on small investment are possible.[21]

As in energy, the stress in agriculture is on the improvement of existing facilities. Capital construction in that sector accounted for only 14 per cent of total state investment in 1979 as compared with 10.7 per cent in 1978, and it seems that for much of the 1980s productivity increases will be effected through better land management and scientific farming.[22] Mechanization is also being encouraged, but at the same time concentrated in selected areas where pay-off is likely to be greatest and fastest.

The Maoist approach of 'grain as the key link' did not prove successful enough to bypass the need for food purchases abroad; the current leadership is promoting specialization in cash crops like cotton, silk, tea, tobacco and fruit, where local conditions permit. Officials may well have accepted a permanent necessity to import grain and the shift to other crops is to satisfy light industry, which requires more raw materials for manufacture of finished goods;[23] these in turn provide exports to be exchanged for capital goods. China's progress is still heavily dependent on the primary sector.

Nevertheless, crucial to economic growth is a balanced relationship between the three sectors of agriculture, light industry and heavy industry. Since the inception of their readjustment policies the Chinese leaders have acted on the assumption that the legitimacy of the CCP, and thus the success of their modernization programme, rest on ability to improve the living standards of the Chinese people. Previously, the Maoist stress on heavy industry had meant neglect of light industry and thus consumer goods. Now, just as the peasantry receive increased income from cash crops, so do city-dwellers earn bonuses as material incentives for higher productivity.

Accordingly, during the years of the Sixth Five-year Plan investment will be transferred from heavy to light industry, a policy which will also economize on energy and raw materials. The intention is to improve supplies of consumer goods, food products and textiles. The most important consumer goods produced in China are electronic products – television sets, cassette recorders, radios and calculators. Goods especially in demand in 1982, for instance, included cigarettes, sugar, wines and spirits, beer, soft drinks, bicycles, sewing-machines and watches. In addition, production of such items as paper, detergents, furniture, clothing and leatherware substantially increased.[24] Consumer-oriented petrochemical products such as chemical fibres, plastics and synthetic rubber are also being promoted.

Certainly, reports indicate a wider array of goods available in China than at any time since 1949. But quantity does not guarantee quality, and even though the current leadership has encouraged the play of market forces – albeit within the state guidelines of a command economy – complacency about a seller's market dies hard and suggests that China is still some way from becoming a consumer-oriented society. Official Chinese press sources have referred to shops and warehouses full of radios, clocks and watches which cannot be sold because of their poor design and low quality.[25]

Recent statements concerning the need for quality improvement reflect rising expectations among the populace, as do government attempts to provide better public amenities like leisure facilities and urban housing as well as other ingredients of the good life. The diversification of consumer goods and the provision of better services are therefore designed to give the population a tangible stake in the success of the modernization programme, while greater mass-media coverage plays a major educational role in creating the skills necessary for further economic advance. Finally, service industries and the expansion of tourism may help solve China's problem of unemployment, especially among urban youth. The growth of light industry is, of course, vital to current economic strategy as it facilitates the accumulation of capital for the future development of heavy industry; in the rural areas profits from consumer goods produced by local industry also provide funds for the purchase of machinery and equipment for the modernization of agriculture.[26]

Thus the current Chinese leadership has stressed light industry and rejected the Maoist idea of autonomous regional development based on the establishment of independent local systems of heavy industry. Excess heavy industrial production capacity in local areas is now being streamlined and, where possible, converted to the production of consumer goods. Medium and small enterprises with poor management and high energy requirements are being closed down. The major focus of reform has been iron and steel plant, recently criticized for waste and inefficiency, and production is now being geared to produce small and medium-sized products like wire rods, sheets and strips.[27]

Although heavy industry's share of total state investment fell from 54.7 per cent in 1978 to 46.8 per cent in 1979 while light industry's proportion rose marginally from 5.4 per cent to 5.8 per cent over the same period, this relative emphasis is only short-term and designed to bring the various economic sectors into a better balance. An efficient agriculture and the local manufacture of consumer goods are making the farming community wealthier, which in turn will stimulate markets for producer goods, thereby driving heavy industry forward.[28] Moreover, in the long term the Chinese leaders will be compelled to boost production, for example, in sectors like steel to satisfy the increasing demands of such interests as the military and transport, which for the time being are likely to remain heavily reliant on imports.

Meanwhile, greater awareness of market forces at home and abroad is leading the Chinese to specialize in those areas of manufacturing – like light industry – to which their human and material resources are at present suited. Thus China's readjustment policies, by exploiting the potential of existing industrial plant, have laid a firmer foundation for foreign trade. At the National Conference on Finance and Trade in

June 1978 the Chinese leaders initiated foreign trade policies
stressing export growth and designed to raise the state's hard
currency earnings, thereby contributing to economic development.

In 1982 the *Beijing Review* outlined the exports which it was
intended to promote. There was, first, a change of policy
regarding minerals, and whereas formerly it was believed that
materials of strategic importance should not be exported,
non-ferrous and rare metals could now be sold abroad.
Secondly, in line with the encouragement of cash crops,
attempts were to be made to increase exports of local speciali-
ties including tea, medicinal herbs, animal products, famous
wild vegetables and preserved fruit. But, although agricultural produce is still prominent, a growing proportion of China's
exports consists of finished goods, as evidenced by emphasis
on machinery and electrical appliances; textiles and other
such light industrial products as porcelain, traditional
Chinese medicines, garments, embroidery and carving are
also being given priority.[29]

In addition, as from 1 January 1982 import duties were
increased on luxury items as well as machinery and equipment which could be manufactured in China, while tariffs
were reduced on rubber, timber, timber products, leather,
pulp, paper and raw materials for the energy industry. These
measures were devised to conserve foreign exchange for
necessary purchases of such items as computers, oil-drilling
equipment and military hardware which as yet could not be
produced in China.[30]

If there are new emphases in the structure of exports,
import policy is also undergoing change. The introduction of
foreign technology by the import of individual machines
which cannot be produced domestically is a considerable
departure from pre-readjustment practice. Construction
during the First Five-year Plan period, for example, was based
mainly on the importation of complete sets of equipment from
the Soviet bloc. Similar policy was followed on a small scale
during the 1960s through relations with Western industrial
countries. From 1973 to 1978 this process was intensified with
complete plant for the chemical, textile, metallurgical and

energy industries introduced from Japan, the United States and Western Europe. The results, however, were neither economically nor technologically ideal; only a third of the projects were completed on time and few have had high operational rates or good returns on investment. So often too much was imported, with similar equipment unnecessarily purchased for different regions of China, resulting in duplication of effort and wastage. This experience has produced a fundamental change of direction; facilities in Chinese enterprises are often adequate for China's purposes but need constant improvement to keep pace with rapid technological change abroad. Thus, if China's technology can be transformed, the full potential of existing facilities will be realized. Higher efficiency will ensure better returns.[31]

The trend, therefore, is towards the introduction of technology from abroad and the accumulation of skills by Chinese experts. The process must, however, be selective, with a view to enhancing technical performance and increasing China's labour productivity, there being no necessity in the immediate future to apply advanced technology to all economic departments. The aim is to utilize the labour force to the full; in the short term, at least, a high level of automation will not be introduced lest it increase the already serious problem of unemployment. For the time being, therefore, a premium will be placed on practical technology which requires less investment, absorbs labour power, and builds up more funds for the state.[32]

At a session of the National People's Congress held in December 1982 Premier Zhao Ziyang warned of a high technological gap emerging between China and Western countries, as the pace of change accelerated. This gap, Chinese leaders believe, can be bridged only by importing equipment with accompanying knowhow, on the principle that productive new technology already developed elsewhere should be suitably adapted and disseminated for application in various industrial sectors. Indispensable, too, is the transfer of knowledge through academic exchanges.[33]

Such knowledge, however, is a precious economic asset, and while the Chinese are pressing for a more rapid transfer of technology the advanced countries of the West have become increasingly concerned about long-term adverse effects on their own export competitiveness and employment situation. At the above-mentioned session of the National People's Congress Zhao Ziyang called for foreign investment; China would thereby acquire much-needed capital from other countries, which would themselves reap a return on such ventures and thus have a stake in China's economic development. There is indeed little alternative to foreign investment, as promotion of domestic consumption to provide material incentives for the workforce places effective limits on the generation of capital exclusively through exploitation of the primary sector.

The main targets for foreign investment during the period 1981 to 1985 reflect readjustment priorities: the intensive development of energy resources, communications and transportation as well as a gradual overhaul of China's existing industrial enterprises, especially those producing goods for export.[34]

The Chinese leaders seek to provide a secure foundation for more rapid economic growth in the second half of the decade and are anxious to avoid any suggestion of foreign economic domination or infringement of China's sovereignty.

At present, for example, China lacks the technical experience, equipment and financial resources to prospect and exploit offshore oil resources on its own but, in inviting participation by Western oil companies, has stipulated that simultaneously Chinese experts should be employed and trained on the job. Similarly, all initial exploration and development costs will be paid by the companies, which will be recompensed through the oil produced. Thus control and ownership will remain with China, thereby ensuring an independent national petroleum industry.[35]

In addition the health of China's economy will depend on increased exports, and foreign investment is being channelled into such industrial areas as Tianjin which, like other coastal regions, is being designated a major export centre, with emphasis on the installation of key facilities in old enterprises to improve product quality.[36]

Readjustment must be understood as a period of transition, laying the foundation for future prosperity, and its success to date will be assessed under the following headings: (i) the improved relationship between the major sectors of the economy; (ii) the betterment of living standards, and (iii) the contribution of foreign trade to China's development.

China has abundant energy resources, with extensive reserves of oil and coal, but most of these are as yet untapped and there is a time-lag between discovery and exploitation. Even though the promotion of light industry and the streamlining of heavy industry were seen as a means of energy conservation, domestic consumption of power is still increasing.

Moreover, 1980 saw a 2.6 per cent decrease in energy production as against 1979, with coal output falling by 2.4 per cent and that for crude oil by 0.2 per cent. Foreign analyses suggest that China could be a net importer of oil by 1990, if current trends continue.[37]

Clearly, China's economic growth will by definition place heavy strains on energy resources and infrastructure during the years to come. But by early 1983 the Chinese leaders' policies had helped to achieve a better balance between economic sectors. At the beginning of readjustment in 1979 light industry's output value increased by 9.6 per cent as compared with heavy industry's gain of 7.7 per cent; in 1980 the former registered a massive growth of 18.4 per cent as against 1.4 per cent in the case of the latter sector. By 1982, however, the picture was slowly changing: heavy industry's output grew in that year by 9.3 per cent, exceeding the planned target of 4 per cent, while light industrial production increased by only 5.1 per cent, although over-fulfilling the projected figure.[38]

Thus, while readjustment policies were designed to expand the supply of consumer goods, heavy industry has at times been performing relatively better than light manufacturing. It was in any case intended at the outset of readjustment that heavy industry would ultimately again be given priority, but already in the short term streamlined existing plant has meant greater efficiency, soon reflected in production figures. In addition, one factor in the levelling off of light industrial growth since 1980 has been rising expectations; quantity of goods has not necessarily meant better quality and consumers are becoming increasingly selective, as some textiles and other manufactured goods with less reputable brand names are being left unsold. Consequently, efficiency-conscious bureaucrats are forcing unsuccessful enterprises to close down or move to new products, in line with the new attention paid to market forces. Furthermore, even though consumer demand continues, individuals are becoming more savings-oriented as banks offer better interest rates. At the end of October 1982, for example, personal savings were 22 per cent higher than at the beginning of the year.

When, at the beginning of readjustment, the workforce was offered incentives for higher output, economic planners sought at the same time to maintain price stability by ensuring that consumer goods production kept pace with rising purchasing power. Chinese statistics must still always be accepted with caution, but official sources estimated that inflation of consumer prices had fallen from 7.5 per cent in 1980 and 2.5 per cent in 1981 to zero in 1982.[39]

A balanced relationship between the heavy and light industrial sectors will nevertheless continue to depend on agriculture providing food for a growing population and cash crops for manufacturing at home as well as export abroad. In 1982 grain output grew by nearly 6 per cent, cotton production by 14 per cent and agricultural productivity in general by 7 per cent over the previous year, such increases being no doubt partly due to favourable weather conditions, import of chemical fertilizer, mechanization, scientific farming and greater investment through bank loans.[40] A more important factor in greater agricultural efficiency, however, has been a new system of family farming whereby peasants can make profits by selling crops in private markets after having fulfilled their grain production quota for the state. There is therefore incentive to increase output.

Official encouragement of market forces in both industry and agriculture has led to marked increases in living standards, even though these have not been shared equally among the population as a whole. Generally, as in other developing countries, the cities are more prosperous than the countryside, but diversification of cash crops is making sections of the peasantry wealthier than many urban workers and city functionaries. One area of China's fertile subtropical province of Guangdong had a *per capita* rural income almost four times the national average.[41]

One effect of readjustment policies has therefore been increased inequality between regions and among individuals, and this process is likely to be intensified as China's greater role in international trade necessarily dictates economic priorities. For example the factories of Shanghai, China's traditional centre of light industry, already account for an eighth of the nation's industrial output, contributing a quarter of total exports, and this pre-eminence is necessarily reflected in the living standards of the city's population.

The contribution to date of foreign economic relations to China's modernization programme is indicated by the changing balance and commodity structure of the country's imports and exports. One justification for readjustment was the need to eliminate foreign trade deficits, which were running at US$1887 million in 1978 and US$3046 million in 1979. By 1981, however, there was a surplus of US$1800 million; the equivalent figure for 1982 was US$4600 million.[42] These statistics would tend to indicate the ccp leaders' decision to import software and single machines as opposed to complete industrial plant; in July 1981, for example, the *Beijing Review* noted how in Xian, capital of Shaanxi Province in Northwest China, the Hongqi Machinery Plant had passed on to 118 factories in the area forty items of advanced industrial techniques, implying technical 'spin-off' to different spheres of production.[43] Such policies have the advantage of requiring cheaper input and producing quicker returns.

Selective importation of technology to increase consumer goods production and render heavy industry more efficient has led to changes in the pattern of China's world trade. Therefore, whereas in the past the Chinese have exported raw materials and agricultural products as well as light industrial goods in exchange for heavy machinery and capital, the trend has recently been reversed. The resulting increase in the proportion of heavy industrial goods exports to China's total exports is shown here:

China's exports by category 1979/1980

	1979 %	1980 %
Heavy industrial products	31.9	39
Agricultural goods	23.1	21.2
Light industrial manufactures/textiles	45	39.8
	100	100

Exports of machinery and power equipment were 37.1 per cent higher in 1980 than in 1979. The corollary of government policy to promote specialization in cash crops is the importation of grain to feed a growing population, especially in the coastal cities; in addition items necessary to raise agricultural yields, together with resources for light industry, are being purchased abroad. Thus in 1980 grain, fats and oils, fertilizer, chemicals, cotton, various fibres and wood pulp accounted for 52.6 per cent of total imports, an increase of 12.2 per cent over 1979, while rolled steel, non-ferrous metals, machinery and instruments represented 27.6 per cent, a drop of 13.5 per cent over the same year.[44] Significantly, products processed from imported materials accounted for more than 40 per cent of China's total export value in 1980.[45] These trends, however, do not preclude future increases in imports of equipment and knowhow to keep pace with advances in technology overseas.

Acceptance of international market forces, as reflected in the commodity structure of China's foreign trade, and stress on material incentives for the workforce to boost output have necessitated changes in state planning and economic institutions. From 1949 until 1979 economic activity followed the Soviet system of public ownership of the means of production. Thus the main focus was not profit in the Western capitalist sense but the promotion of industrial and agricultural output to satisfy the basic needs of state and society. Throughout 1978, however, newly rehabilitated economists began to advocate managing the economy through market forces and fiscal measures instead of administrative planning alone. This meant that while the structure of the command economy would not be completely dismantled, greater weight was to be given to quality control and consumer choice.

This policy created a commitment to private enterprise in industry reminiscent of New Democracy in the early 1950s, when Mao advocated a united front in the form of economic collaboration between the CCP and those capitalists inherited from the Guomindang regime who alone at that time had the experience to run a modern industrial enterprise. Chinese leaders have recently implied that the stage of New Democracy has not yet been completed.[46] Thus, in 1981, the CCP rehabilitated 700,000 former businessmen who had been denounced as exploiters in the 1960s and 1970s, especially at the height of the Cultural Revolution; their express intention being to utilize all available skills to create the preconditions for the transition to socialism. In the present Chinese leaders' view, therefore, capitalism is a means to a socialist end, but for many years to come long-term social goals will be sacrificed in the interests of a developing economy. There are moves away from the two models of the past: the excessively centralized Soviet First Five-year Plan and the enhanced mass mobilization of the Great Leap Forward and the Cultural Revolution. In one respect, of course, Chinese society is moving closer to its Soviet counterpart with the emergence of a technocratic élite increasingly able to bargain with society for the price of its services.

Material incentives, individual initiative and social inequality are being seen as the *sine qua non* of economic development; creation of wealth must necessarily precede its distribution. While the CCP still brooks no organized opposition to its policies, personal performance in whatever field of endeavour is now considered more crucial than political commitment *per se*, and in the words of Deng Xiaoping, 'it does not matter whether the cat is black or white as long as it catches mice'.

Encouragement of market forces within the framework of a command economy has necessitated two major adjustments in the planning mechanism: (i) the changing role of the banks, and (ii) decentralization, allowing greater initiative to local authorities and production units, both industrial and agricultural.

Whereas, before readjustment, banks had been responsible for distributing funds allocated by the state, they are now playing a greater role in directing capital investment on the criterion of profitability.

Even more significant for China's future prosperity is the new balance of economic power between central and local governments, as defined in a State Council circular of February 1980. Crucial heavy industries – for example those related to national defence – are still subject to central planning and control, while other state-run sectors come under varying degrees of jurisdiction from central and local government. Under the new economic reforms the central government will continue to be guaranteed a large percentage of the nation's total revenues from industrial enterprises, but local economic powers have been reinforced and the scope of local plans widened.

These policies of limited devolution are a reaction against what is now seen as over-centralization in the past and have been designed to give local governments a greater stake in the profitability of enterprises under their jurisdiction. Similarly, attempts have been made to rationalize enterprise management to achieve greater accountability regarding profits and losses. Formerly, technical experts were often subordinate to party secretaries, but now a line is drawn between political duties involving moral exhortation and the major concern of increasing production, with responsibility being delegated to the technologically oriented factory managers, albeit under overall Party Committee leadership.

Planning is being more closely related to the laws of supply and demand. After fulfilling state targets enterprise management may produce more goods in response to public demand, and set its own prices. In addition, enterprises are permitted to retain a fixed percentage of their profits for reinvestment or repayment of loans, and the state no longer subsidizes losses.[47] Market forces also operate in the transfer of raw materials and components between enterprises; this is now on a contractual basis rather than through state-determined allocation, even though certain restrictions still apply to materials of national importance in short supply.[48]

More crucial to China's modernization programme, however, than the reform of economic institutions is the motivation of the workforce. From 1949 to 1979 manpower was directed by the state to various industrial sectors and given the so-called 'iron rice-bowl'. In 1980 enterprise management was given the right, on an experimental basis, to select, punish and dismiss workers. Further incentives to improve efficiency and raise output have included authority to provide cash incentives and adjust wage levels according to performance, although within a range approved by the central government.

Although many observers consider them as steps in the right direction, these measures must nevertheless be regarded as experimental. The CCP leaders introduced rationalization in selected areas before extending the policy to the country as a whole, and within a year ten enterprises in Sichuan Province were reported to have raised their profits by 61 per cent.[49]

But old attitudes die hard and institutional reforms do not immediately change attitudes born of entrenched vested interests. In spite of their conversion to the idea of market forces, China's government economists still continue to think in terms of central planning; ministry officials have been reluctant to relinquish control over such key factors as manning levels, raw material costs, power supplies, prices and profits.[50] There have been problems too with bonus systems which are often awarded to all workers, thereby reducing intended incentive. It seems unlikely that the reform of industrial enterprises introduced during the years of readjustment will be reversed, but the need to ensure stability during a period of transition suggests that certain elements of central planning may be reinforced in the short term.

Agriculture and light industry in the countryside belong to what is known as the system of collective ownership as opposed to the state sector, and are by their very nature more distant from direct government control than, for example, urban heavy industry, although Party Committees at various levels ensure compliance with national plans. Since 1978 reforms in the management of the agricultural sector have nevertheless followed a pattern similar to changes in industry, with production units granted greater autonomy in the interests of increased output. As in industrial enterprises, decisions are now guided by economic indicators rather than being subject to administrative orders. The administrative powers of the people's communes have been transferred to the local township and most of their economic powers given to production teams. Team leadership, however, no longer manages farming directly but contracts, with team members, as individuals or families, for the fulfilment of production targets. To provide incentives for the peasants every farming task is given a quotient of work points. This system, on which payment is calculated, is devised at production brigade level. After team members have met their assigned quotas of, for example, grain for allocation to the state, they are free to plant other crops. Some products may be sold on the free market by the peasants themselves. In addition, individual households can gain further income from the sale of such foodstuffs as vegetables and poultry produced on their private plots, the permitted size of which has been recently increased, thereby improving the diet of city residents.[51]

Originally the people's communes were conceived of as a 'short cut' in the development process, with increased agricultural production through economies of scale seen as facilitating local self-sufficiency and the industrialization of the countryside. Since readjustment the teams, farming families or even individuals, in addition to their agricultural function, have been encouraged to earn further income and accumulate capital by establishing their own industrial enterprises in sectors like food-processing, and repair as well as manufacture of agricultural equipment. By 1982 such enterprises, run by a single team or teams in collaboration, outnumbered those operated at commune and brigade levels. Significantly, however, initiative for such departures often comes from higher authorities – like county Party Committees – which can offer needed credit and technological input, thus placing constraints on independent entrepreneurship. Scarce energy resources also restrict the creation of local industry in the countryside.[52]

Therefore, while greater team autonomy and concomitant material incentives for increased output are likely to remain, further progress in the countryside may well depend on funds for mechanization, capital construction and technological change, resources which can come only from higher authorities – the state sector through the central planning agencies or via local government. Moreover, in the last analysis, China's future economic development will rest on the ability of political leadership to inculcate those values best attuned to the modernization process.

4 Sino–Japanese Partnership: Trade and economic co-operation

China is no exception to the general rule that governments are to a greater or lesser extent accountable to their peoples; reform of the Chinese foreign trade system to compete more effectively on international markets and promote Sino–Japanese economic co-operation must be balanced against social imperatives and potentially conflicting cultural factors at home. Only if their living standards are improved will China's people as a whole be convinced that the current leadership's economic policies are necessary and just; and while enterprise and local autonomy are intended as incentive to produce wealth, social stability demands that individual and regional disparities in wealth be kept within bounds.

Thus recent reforms of China's foreign trade system reflect the need to retain centralized control and guidance while giving considerable initiative to provinces and individual industrial concerns. Decentralization does not mean 'privatization', as all overseas business is subject to a central authority, but is intended to promote modernization policies by increasing foreign trade. Central guidance is guaranteed by the recently reconstituted Ministry of Foreign Economic Relations and Trade, which has established representative offices in Shanghai, Tianjin, Dalian and Guangzhou, designed to strengthen administrative control over external trade, and through a Ministry presence in major ports to streamline procedures, thus facilitating export flow. Unified implementation of national policy is thereby maintained but rigidity of centralized management eliminated. Similarly, the head offices of a number of import and export corporations under the Ministry of Foreign Economic Relations determine dealings in a number of important commodities like finished petroleum products and metal ores subject to national or international controls. Thus local government authorities are not allowed to export these items; likewise, such raw material imports as steel and cotton require licences.

Most foreign commercial business, however, is handled by coastal or local trading corporations as well as newly constituted bodies under other state ministries. Foreign trade corporations have been set up in, for example, the municipalities of Beijing, Tianjin and Shanghai, in addition to the provinces of Guangdong, Fujian, Liaoning and Hebei. These corporations handle their own imports and exports as well as related transport, warehousing, packaging and advertising. As of late 1980, for instance, Sichuan had eight such bodies dealing in products like textiles, tea, animal by-products and foodstuffs. Additionally, there are specialized trading corporations under, for instance, the Ministries of Machine Building and Metallurgy, controlling relevant sectors of overriding national importance.

Generally speaking, then, the export of locally produced commodities may be handled by the provinces themselves, and similar initiative has also been, to a limited extent, devolved to industrial enterprises. Before the early 1980s producers had no direct contact with clients abroad, transactions being handled by foreign trade departments; but it is now considered crucial for individual enterprises to seek foreign customers' specifications regarding quality and design. A case in point is the porcelain plant in Hunan's Liling County, which has negotiated its own contracts with foreign companies instead of acting through a state intermediary.[1] Moreover, in economic sectors where the state still does play a role in negotiation, attempts are being made to achieve better co-ordination as, for example, between the Shanghai shipyard and the China Machinery Import and Export Corporation.

Nevertheless, however much independent initiative is devolved to localities and enterprises, optimum conditions for overseas trade and foreign investment in China can be created only at national level, with central government maintaining an overall view of economic progress. State mechanisms of control are thus necessary not only because of the demands of a developing economy but to keep excessive regional income disparity in check, lest rising expectations, fuelled by popular exposure to Western tastes through media and tourism, prove unacceptably divisive.

In this context of supervision four major bodies may be cited. The China Council for the Promotion of International Trade, while promoting close ties with China's industries and trading corporations, carries out extensive public relations work abroad, organizing exhibitions at home and overseas, publishing advertising literature and so presenting China's goods to the world. The Council also performs a reconnaissance function by distributing information on new products so that Chinese buyers may keep abreast of major developments in international markets. It is also active in the legal sphere, handling such matters as trade-mark registration and issuing documents.[2]

To ensure that Chinese products are competitive, the China National Import and Export Commodities Inspection Corporation conducts surveys of goods being sent abroad, on commission from foreign business firms. Consulting services are also offered to protect the interests of overseas traders and thereby enhance China's credibility as a supplier.

In a centrally planned economy like China's, the rapid expansion of foreign trade by both national and local government authorities has meant the retention of import and export controls, with licences being granted by the Foreign Trade Administration Bureau, which also allocates export quotas like those on spun and woven products set by a recent agreement with the United States.

Economic co-operation, as well as trade, will play a crucial role in China's modernization programme, and to utilize foreign funds better the State Council has established the China International Trust and Investment Corporation as a liaison body for introducing overseas investors to interested leaders in economic organs and industrial enterprises, with concomitant corporations being set up in certain provinces and cities.

China's maritime provinces, the main beneficiaries of self-management authority, already account for almost half of China's total industrial output and three-quarters of the country's total export trade, and such areas will undoubtedly become even more advantaged *vis-à-vis* the rest of the country, given that they are being designated as zones for boosting future exports. Moreover, in addition to a greater say in the promotion of foreign trade, they have been granted the right to import technology and undertake co-operative industrial ventures with overseas companies, although on the understanding that the overall national interest is protected.

The value change which the CCP leaders have sought to introduce through foreign trade reform is, however, proving a mixed blessing, and institutional mechanisms like the four discussed above have been clearly insufficient alone to prevent individual provinces and enterprises enriching themselves at the expense of the wider public interest. That privileges have been abused is indicated by reports in the Chinese press which are replete with examples of misuse of foreign exchange earned from overseas trade.

Authorities in coastal Guangdong, abundant in agricultural resources, were stated to have spent little of this income in 1981 on transforming other industries and communications in the less well-endowed areas of the province; on the contrary much foreign currency had been sold at a huge profit, and at two or three times the official rate, to other interior provinces and municipalities desperately in need of it, thereby creating wealth differentials both within and between regions.[3]

Other sources suggest even more serious side-effects. Local autonomy has meant inadequate management of foreign exchange reserves, to the detriment of the national economy. Investment has been subject to both poor co-ordination of economic planning among local authorities and excessive imports of attractive consumer goods. In summary, foreign currency is frequently over-concentrated at local level, with resulting falls in remission of such revenue to central government.[4]

It was to curb such excesses that the State General Administration of Exchange Control and its regional branches were set up; these bodies are closely associated with the Bank of China. Although local state organs and enterprises are permitted to retain a certain percentage of foreign currency earned, for example, through exports as payment for imports, under the supervision of the Bank of China foreign exchange laws forbid deposits of overseas currency abroad, and similar rules apply to economic concerns established by China in foreign countries.

Such laws, however, are as much directed towards China's foreign partners; the Chinese leaders have never ceased to condemn, in United Nations forums and elsewhere, what they see as the unfair terms of trade exacted from the developing states by the developed countries. Similarly, the Chinese view Western investment in the Third World as a form of neocolonialism or economic domination and, while seeking to convince countries like Japan of their sincerity in offering generous conditions for foreign investors, nevertheless wish to stop them extracting excessive profit and taking advantage of China's backwardness.

It is against this background of value change and foreign trade reform that the CCP leaders are soliciting economic co-operation from Japan. Future economic growth, however, will initially depend on the exploitation of China's abundant energy resources and the expansion of the physical infrastructure, that is, the transportation and communication systems. But if the Chinese wish to avoid undue dependence on any one foreign investor, their major partners in resource development, the Japanese, are determined to diversify their sources of raw material supply. A cornerstone of Japan's post-war economically oriented foreign policy has been omnidirectional diplomacy. The Japanese have accordingly sought to steer a middle course between their neighbours, China and the Soviet Union, seeking to maintain the current fragile balance of power. Since the mid-1960s they have been active in assisting the development of Soviet Siberian energy resources but at the same time they are careful not to increase Chinese leaders' fears concerning China's national security.

The Chinese are in any case keen to preserve a balance between domestic power generation needs on the one hand

and energy exports, for example to Japan, on the other. This is true of both oil and coal; the country's oil exports are expected to fall over the next few years because of declining production and growing domestic demand, despite recently launched conservation programmes and the increased use of coal as well as other energy resources. Old oil-fields have been worked to the limit and new sites are only just coming into production.

Most power generation in China comes from coal, placing limits on the amount that may be sold, for instance, to major buyers like Japanese steel-makers. Nuclear power is yet to be used on any significant scale. Thus not all energy resources exploitable with the aid of Japanese investment and technology will be available to satisfy Japan's immediate needs. In concluding co-operation agreements with China, however, the Japanese are indicating willingness to take short-term risks for pay-off in the long run.

Of course, Japanese economic co-operation is not entirely disinterested, as energy from China provides Japan with supplies alternative to those from politically volatile areas of the world like the Middle East. By the terms of a long-term bilateral trade agreement signed in 1978 the Chinese promised to deliver ten million tons of coal to Japan by 1985, a deal made possible by a recent Japanese loan to develop seven new mines. In July 1981 the governmental Export-Import Bank of Japan contracted with the Bank of China to extend seven untied loans worth 42,000 million yen (US$140 million) for the development of both coal and petroleum resources for subsequent export to Japan; oil-prospecting has been heavily concentrated at the west of Bohai Bay in the Yellow Sea.[5]

In spite of massive reserves, especially of coal, China's energy exports are still being inhibited by inadequate transportation facilities. Already, expansion and improvement of railways and harbour facilities is being financed by Japan's Overseas Economic Co-operation Fund (OECF) loans. On completion of a new railway, for example, great quantities of coal will be carried from the northern province of Shanxi to the port of Qinhuangdao, which is itself being expanded under the same agreement. Japanese terms to date have been generous: a fiscal 1979 OECF yen credit involved only 3 per cent interest, with repayment over thirty years and a ten-year grace period.[6]

At the time of writing, the bulk of Japanese loans is being devoted to improvements and expansion of China's physical infrastructure. Moreover, the CCP's readjustment programme in fact places limits on Japanese exports for other Chinese economic sectors because stress is now being laid on updating existing industrial capacity rather than on the purchase of new plant. The keynote is greater efficiency: advanced technology will be adopted and adapted, scientific management introduced, product quality upgraded, manufacturing costs reduced, technical personnel retrained and exports increased and made more competitive.

In the long term, however, the development of China's industry will stimulate Japan's exports. Furthermore, such is the level of China's technology that the Japanese will not immediately suffer from Chinese competition on world markets, and China's leaders have recently been emphasizing those sectors of light industry virtually abandoned by Japan in the last two decades. Third World countries, however, may well find China a major competitor in the years to come.

Thus Sino–Japanese co-operation in the modernization of factories stems from the Chinese leaders' decision to revamp existing plant, for instance in heavy industry, and the absence of alternative lucrative projects in China. Attention is therefore being focused on solving technological problems involved in the production process.[7]

Technical co-operation is, of course, never one-sided; there is continual 'spin-off' of knowledge for Japanese industry, as witnessed, for instance, by the contributions of both sides at the First China–Japan Symposium on steel-making, held in Beijing during September 1981 and sponsored by the Chinese Society of Metals and the Iron and Steel Institute of Japan. Similarly, the Japan–China Industrial Technical Exchange Association, with over twenty small and medium-sized Japanese enterprises as members, established in Tokyo in March 1982, is intended to enhance technology and administration in both countries by exchanging post-graduate trainees, enterprise personnel and experience with industrial production techniques. Japanese engineers are being sent to many of the 380,000 smaller plants, especially textile and light industrial concerns around major cities like Beijing and Shanghai, which the ccp leaders have slated for productivity improvement.

One way in which the Chinese leaders can show tangible improvements in living standards is by increasing the availability of good-quality consumer products. In this context Matsushita Electric of Japan is providing the Yangkou Washing-Machine General Plant in Liaoning with the technical guidance to attain Japanese quality levels. Likewise, in July 1981 a new colour assembly line, built by the National Electric Company of Japan, opened at the Beijing Television Factory and during a six-month trial period Japanese specialists advised on processes.

In addition, with diversification of consumer taste, the Japanese are installing plant for the processing of foodstuffs, as demonstrated by the construction of China's first integrated margarine and shortening plant.

Agriculture, like light industry, is one of the Chinese leaders' current priorities and the Japanese, long since pioneers in raising crop yields for Southeast Asian countries, have received orders for agricultural equipment from China's National Machinery Import and Export Corporation. A training centre for mechanized rice cultivation has been established, with technical guidance from Japan and funding from China. In addition, the two countries are undertaking a joint survey of agricultural resources in the northeastern province of Heilongjiang.

Information retrieval systems are a key to future efficiency in China's economy as a whole, and this has been reflected in the establishment of the Sino–Japanese Computer Software Centre by the China Computer Technical Service Corporation and the Nippon Electric Corporation. This is designed to train Chinese technicians, instruct enterprise managers in basic knowledge, and facilitate the eventual production of new models. Computer systems are being provided by the Japanese, with China contributing managerial staff and accommodation.[8]

In banking, computer technology is especially relevant to cope with fast business expansion; in July 1981 the Tokai Bank of Nagoya, having acquired the same system from Hitachi, contracted to supply the Bank of China with utilization knowhow and train Chinese technicians in Japan.

Only through such acquisition of foreign technology will the Chinese be able to enhance export potential and gain greater access to overseas markets. To improve the quality of exports, Japanese aid is being enlisted through a broader form of economic co-operation – compensation trade, an arrangement by which the Chinese pay for up-to-date capital equipment through export of manufactures. In following trade-mark specification, the Chinese become aware of modern design and fashion trends. In turn, the foreign exchange earned facilitates further imports of industrial plant from Japan and elsewhere.

Although, as in other aspects of foreign trade relations, limited autonomy has been granted to individual provinces, major cities and enterprises, central control is retained by the Export-Import Corporations under the State Council. Thus foreign firms wishing to engage in compensation trade contact these corporations or their regional branches, which forward proposals to industrial ministries for negotiation. The Chinese foreign trade corporations concerned have been responsible for signing and helping to implement contracts agreed upon. The provinces of Guangdong and Fujian, however, have the authority to conclude compensation trade deals up to a certain value – in 1982 the prevailing figure being US$5 million – without the prior approval of central government organs. In fact, very few contracts to date have exceeded this value. Similarly China's three largest cities, Beijing, Shanghai and Tianjin, have authority to approve deals worth up to US$3 million, the ceiling for other provinces being one million US dollars. As incentives for higher productivity, enterprises are entitled to keep all profits in Renminbi (Chinese currency) derived from domestic sales and 30 per cent of any foreign exchange earnings accruing from exports. Any balance of foreign exchange profit is remitted to the provincial governments, which turn over a fixed amount annually to the central authorities. In 1982, for instance, Guangdong remitted about US$1000 million in profit, but above the set quota was allowed to keep 70 per cent of its foreign exchange earnings. Quotas remitted are to be periodically adjusted according to trade fluctuation.

Thus in the immediate term only the coastal regions and the major cities will be enriched, even if in the long run it is intended that the revenue remitted and the technology disseminated as a result of compensation deals will benefit the whole of China.

A notable example of compensation trade has been the agreement for production of pyjamas concluded in mid-1978 between Itoman Limited, a medium-sized Japanese trading firm, and the Shanghai branch of the China Textile Import and Export Corporation. While the Japanese side have provided technicians and equipment the basic raw material, cotton, has been purchased on the local market and the products given Itoman's brand name. The Japanese are doubly advantaged: because of Chinese wage levels, the price of first shipments reaching Japan in mid-1978 was lower than the equivalent cost of similar textiles being produced for Japan's companies in South Korea and Taiwan; moreover, in view of high transportation costs, the compensation formula is not really a viable proposition for Japan's competitors in Western Europe.

Although by the end of 1979 some 140 contracts had been signed and further deals have since followed, weaknesses inherent in the Chinese economy, as well as Japanese reservations, put constraints on the development of compensation trade. Management reform in China's export and import corporations has brought its own problems, stemming from the expansion of local self-management authority: it is now more difficult, for example, to combine materials available in Shanghai with similar sources in Beijing. There is also the old question of quality control: in the textile industry, for instance, skills have been of a high order but this is not necessarily true of other industries. In addition, capitalist ways of operating have some tradition in Shanghai and Guangdong, but these ideas have yet to gain complete favour in Beijing. Despite Japanese technical assistance there are still massive power shortages, with factories operating only two or three days a week. Finally, while the Japanese might wish to see the goods produced through compensation trade sold on domestic markets the CCP leaders, for their part, have sought to export to third countries, thereby protecting other sectors of light industry not yet benefiting from new Japanese technology during this period of economic transition, and also increasing China's foreign exchange earnings. Nevertheless, in 1984 there were signs that the Chinese were relaxing this condition whereby such goods have to be marketed outside China – a Japanese manufacturer, for example, being permitted to sell products to satisfy the Chinese domestic market and stem the purchase of expensive imports. The Japanese in any case no doubt anticipate that the risks they now take will ultimately pay off in increased Chinese purchases of capital plant for all sectors of China's economy.

If, under the terms of compensation trade, the Chinese eventually acquire ownership of, for instance, Japanese equipment in return for goods produced, joint ventures will become one framework for longer-term foreign investment in China's economic development.

Four major national bodies have ensured central government control of joint ventures: responsibility for approving or rejecting applications lies with the Foreign Investment Commission; the China International Trust and Investment Corporation serves as a business organization co-ordinating the use of overseas capital and technology, sometimes itself investing both inside and outside China; and the finance required of the Chinese side is channelled through the People's Construction Bank of China. Finally, the General Administration for Industry and Commerce and its provincial bureaux are authorized to supervise and inspect the joint ventures in operation. In accordance, however, with the policy of local autonomy, authority for approving small and medium-sized joint ventures is being gradually delegated to individual ministries of the central government and to provinces, especially Guangdong and Fujian.

A joint venture involves foreign investors who, by Chinese

law, must have at least a 25 per cent stake in the overall investment and thus become shareholders. They provide necessary funds for construction and equipment, while the Chinese side contribute land, buildings and offices which in monetary terms become part of the enterprise's capital stock. Both sides participate in management.

The Chinese leaders have offered considerable incentives to foreign investors through tax concessions and liberal regulations on the remission of profits abroad, but they are equally determined to have as much income as possible derived from foreign ventures reinvested in China. Accordingly, both Chinese and foreign partners pay income tax at the rate of 30 per cent. Moreover, a sum equivalent to 10 per cent of that 30 per cent is paid as a levy to the relevant local government. As further encouragement, newly established joint ventures scheduled to operate for ten years or more may be exempted from tax in the first profit-making year and allowed a 50 per cent reduction for the next two years. Special tax incentives are in operation for low-profit ventures in agriculture, forestry or economically underdeveloped areas of China. In addition, on approval by the Bank of China, foreign participants in joint ventures may remit abroad their share of net profit, on payment of an additional income tax of 10 per cent.[9]

By mid-1981 a total of 131 joint ventures using Chinese and foreign capital had opened accounts, as required by law, with the Bank of China; their areas of interest reflected the CCP's economic readjustment priorities, being concentrated in energy, light industry, tourism, communications, service trades and agriculture. In general, emphasis has been on small and medium-sized projects, transforming and increasing the potential of existing facilities as well as prospecting for new energy resources.

Several cases will serve to indicate Japan's growing involvement in joint ventures and that role is greater than at first sight, as many similarly active Hong Kong firms have close associations with Japanese companies. Joint development of China's oil resources was first mooted during the visit of a Japanese Ministry of Trade and Industry (MITI) mission in late 1974, and after the establishment of the Japan–China Oil

Development Corporation, a contract was signed between the two governments during May 1980 on prospecting in the southern and western parts of the Bohai Sea. In addition to China's stake, funds were invested by the Japan National Oil Corporation and forty-seven Japanese companies concerned with petroleum development, oil-refining, electric power and the steel industry. Of the development fund 49 per cent was to be contributed by the Japan-China Oil Development Corporation, a further 49 per cent by China via a Japanese Export Import Bank loan, and the final 2 per cent by the Chinese side in the form of Renminbi currency. Initial survey costs in the Bohai Sea were to be borne by Japan.[10] Drilling of the first production oil-well under the above agreement began in April 1982 at the Chengbei oil-field in the Bohai Sea.

Although an alternative source of power in the foreseeable future, Chinese oil will satisfy only a tiny percentage of Japan's needs in the immediate term. It will, however, be a secure source; assuming continuing political stability in China, the Chinese leaders seem unlikely to jeopardize co-operation in other fields by nationalizing Japan's oil investment, a practice not unknown elsewhere in the Third World. The Chinese, for their part, wish to maintain control over a precious economic asset and a state body, the China National Offshore Oil Corporation (CNOOC), is officially in charge of exploiting and marketing offshore petroleum sources, albeit in co-operation with foreign enterprises. Thus it is envisaged that the CNOOC will take over production operations when conditions permit. Even more crucial to China than investment is expertise, and in the course of operations Chinese personnel must be employed in increasing proportions as they gain necessary experience, with a view to staffing an independent oil industry. Similarly, provided that they are competitive in terms of efficiency, quality and pricing, Chinese engineering companies, equipment and services will receive preference. Some of the oil produced will be set aside for China, with the remainder allotted to repay both parties' investment plus interest. In line with legislation relating to joint ventures, the foreign company may export the petroleum allocated as its share and remit profits abroad.[11]

Other economic sectors are also benefiting from an infusion of Japanese technology and experience through joint ventures. For instance, the China Orient Leasing Company Limited was officially inaugurated in early 1981, with the China International Trust and Investment Corporation, the Beijing Electromechanical Company Limited, and the Japan Orient Leasing Company entering into partnership to hire out equipment and facilities for light industry, transport and agriculture, as well as to provide an up-to-date information service for Chinese clients. The enterprise was capitalized at US$3 million; the Beijing company held 30 per cent, the Investment Corporation 20 per cent and the Japanese side 50 per cent of the total stake.[12]

Similarly, Sino–Japanese liaison bodies have been set up to promote economic co-operation: in August 1982 the Shoko Chukin Bank of Japan signed a contract with the Liaoning branch of the China Trust and Investment Corporation under which both parties would introduce appropriate companies for joint ventures, exchanging information and facilitating capital procurement. The bank is also assisting smaller Japanese companies to start joint ventures in the provinces of Guangdong and Fujian.[13]

Most joint ventures to date have been in light industry, which promises the quickest returns in job creation and production of consumer goods for the domestic and foreign markets. Facilities are being improved to make traditional industries more efficient, an instance being the new woollen mill jointly run by the Inner Mongolian Textile Corporation and the Japanese firm Mitsui, and located in one of China's top cashmere-producing areas. To remain competitive in world markets, however, the Chinese, like the Japanese before them, must diversify their range of products and move into new areas like electronics. Inaugurated in 1981, the Fujian Hitachi Television Company Limited is scheduled to produce 200,000 14-inch and 20-inch colour television sets and 180,000 12-inch black-and-white sets per year. Initially, they are being sold mainly in China but eventually over half of them will be exported. Major shareholders are the Hitachi Corporation with a 38 per cent share and the Fujian Electrical Import and

Export Corporation with a 40 per cent stake. The term of the joint venture is fifteen years and both sides are represented on the Board of Directors.[14]

Finally tourism, potentially a great foreign exchange earner, is also providing a fertile field for co-operation; the Fujian Province Investment Enterprise Company, with a 51 per cent holding, and the Japanese firm Kato Bussan, with a 49 per cent share, have formed a joint venture for hotel construction and management in Fujian City.[15]

China, however, has as yet only a limited number of experienced businessmen who can successfully participate in joint ventures, and her leaders are now beginning to encourage the establishment on Chinese soil of enterprises completely owned by foreigners. Significantly these new bodies, like many of the compensation arrangements and joint ventures, will in the main be established in the coastal provinces of Guangdong and Fujian, particularly within the Special Economic Zones now being designated by the CCP as economic pace-setters for the rest of China. Before discussing these zones, however, a brief introduction is necessary.

In spite of their new openness to the outside world on economic grounds, the Chinese leaders are still dedicated in the long run to the eventual creation of an egalitarian Communist society. They are therefore apprehensive about possible undesirable capitalist influences, especially on those leaders and workers having close association with foreigners in the new Special Economic Zones. They have, then, been at pains to justify the new arrangements in terms of Marxist-Leninist doctrine in order to prevent bribery and corruption, the most obvious signs of cultural pollution from the West, including Japan.

In June 1981 a Chinese academic journal quoted the Soviet leader Lenin, who in the 1920s was forced to retreat from radical policies and institute the so-called New Economic Policy which offered limited concessions to private enterprise in the interests of economic stability and growth. There is also a Chinese precedent. In 1940, nine years before the Communist accession to power, Mao Zedong had written his treatise 'On New Democracy'. China, he said, was as yet an economically backward country relying on subsistence agriculture, possessing little industry except on the coast, and only a tiny industrial proletariat.

Thus only with the expertise of industrialists and entrepreneurs from the old society could China's industries be developed so that the conditions for the creation of a socialist society could be met. Learning from the Soviet experience, as propounded by Lenin, the CCP leaders retained the services of the old capitalists, first as enterprise owners subject to state guidance and fiscal control, and then by the late 1950s as salaried officials while the bulk of Chinese industry was gradually nationalized. The ultimate aim had always been the transformation of private enterprise into the state sector.

The CCP was, however, discerning in its choice of partners; only the so-called 'national capitalists' who claimed to have suffered from the economic policies of the Guomindang – the previous rulers – and so expressed a willingness to accept the new regime, and whose activities could be restricted, were seen as dependable. But those industrialists too closely associated with the old order were excluded from the new arrangements. This CCP-dominated partnership with such capitalists has remained a precedent for contemporary collaboration with traders and entrepreneurs from abroad.

Special Economic Zones are therefore conceived of as a broader arena for the utilization of foreign investment and the acquisition of technology, as well as schools for personnel training, whether in production itself, scientific management, or marketing of goods.

Thus in the Marxist-Leninist categories of the Chinese leaders, the joint enterprises established in these zones are ideologically quite respectable, as they represent a partnership with foreign capital which is nevertheless under direct state control. The interests of the Chinese people are looked after and any neocolonialist domination is thereby precluded. Ideological education of the Chinese working in the zones will, however, always remain crucially necessary.[16]

The economic advantages for China may well outweigh the dangers of cultural pollution. The CCP leaders envisage that the Special Economic Zones will act as a testing ground for the reform of China's economic system as a whole, and eventually some foreign capital and advanced technology will be transferred to other parts of the country. Light industrial joint ventures will also provide work for unemployed youth.

Once again inducements are being offered to foreign firms; administrative delays in approving new enterprises in the Special Economic Zones have been reduced and financial incentives introduced. In 1980 the *Beijing Review*, in quoting the newly formulated regulations, gave the rate of income tax to be paid by the enterprises in the zones as 15 per cent, with preferential treatment given to those established within two years, ventures with an investment of US$5 million or more, and plants involving specified higher technologies. In addition spare parts and raw materials would be exempted from import duties. As in the case of joint ventures elsewhere in China foreign businessmen, after paying income tax, would be allowed to remit abroad profits and salaries through a zone's banks.

It was, however, stipulated that products were intended for the international market; enterprises wishing to sell in China would require the approval of the administration in charge of the zone, itself responsible to the provincial government. Customs dues were then to be paid. Finally, joint ventures would be given favourable consideration in such matters as land rent, tenancy and the length of lease.[17]

Progress in the Special Economic Zones to date will now be examined. Most investors have been overseas Chinese businessmen from Hong Kong and Macao and, as many of their firms are subsidiaries of Japanese companies, the Japanese stake is greater than at first sight. Sharing a common culture with the Chinese leaders, they serve as perfect go-betweens for the Japanese. Results to date have been mixed, and while the CCP leaders and the Japanese are taking a long perspective, some Hong Kong businessmen have often been accused of taking a short-term view, seeing the zones as an opportunity for property speculation or a site where cheap outdated machinery may be utilized and low wages paid to Chinese workers.

Shenzhen, the biggest zone, covering an area of 28 square

miles north of Hong Kong's New Territories, has a resident
population of about 80,000, in addition to which there are
40,000 construction workers. Chinese officials suggest that the
population could rise to 800,000 by the turn of the century.
Under 10 per cent of foreign investment in Shenzhen is
devoted to industrial projects but 70 per cent is committed to
the development of offices, hotels, and other tourist facilities
which some overseas investors believe offer quick returns. No
doubt, however, these developments will eventually bear fruit
for China, as will improvement and expansion of antiquated
infra-structure now in progress in the zones, for which
thousands of millions of US$ worth of Chinese funds have
been earmarked. Such spending, together with imported
industrial equipment of equivalent value, is the only way to
realize the ambitious export targets now being mooted. The
Chinese leaders intend to lay the foundation for future
economic growth; given better communications, Chinese
leaders believe that Shenzhen will develop into an oil city. The
wealth created in the zone will in turn promote better services
and facilities in the seaboard areas of Guangdong and set off a
chain reaction of development in all economic sectors,
increasing the prosperity of China as a whole.[18]

By 1984 the Chinese leaders were sufficiently impressed
with such progress to designate fourteen more coastal cities as
Special Economic Zones, including such major centres as
Dalian, Tianjin and Shanghai.

In his report to the Sixth National People's Congress in
May of that year China's Premier, Zhao Ziyang, offered
additional inducements to foreign entrepreneurs: those overseas investors who provided the zones with advanced technology were to be given further tax incentives and permitted to
sell a proportion of the goods produced in joint ventures on
the Chinese domestic market.

The future of Hong Kong, Macao and Taiwan, however,
casts a long shadow over such co-operation. It is perhaps
significant that the main Special Economic Zones lie in the
southern provinces of Guangdong and Fujian, close to Hong
Kong and the Portuguese enclave, Macao; and one of them is
opposite Taiwan, the seat of the Guomindang, the Chinese

Nationalists, who claim to be the government of the whole of China. While, as already mentioned, the immediate purpose of the zones is to attract foreign investment, the CCP leaders undoubtedly regard them as a means by which the three disputed areas could be reintegrated into the Chinese People's Republic.

For many years the Chinese leaders have sought to woo political figures and prominent industrialists on the island of Taiwan with offers of high position and lucrative business opportunities, on terms similar to those used to control China mainland capitalists during the 1950s. Naturally enough, Chinese Nationalist leaders have rejected such blandishments out of hand as partnership on Communist terms, but similar inducements are now being subtly offered to Hong Kong Chinese businessmen, especially in the context of negotiations concerning the colony's fate after 1997, when nine-tenths of its territory is due to revert to the sovereignty of China's government under the terms of the original treaty.

At the time of writing, Sino–British negotiations have ended in a compromise by which China will regain sovereignty over Hong Kong in 1997, with the wishes of its inhabitants taken account of in a Chinese promise allowing them to retain their free society and capitalist economy for a transitional period of fifty years.

Such promises are, of course, yet to be fully tested and no doubt many Hong Kong businessmen have transferred their funds from the colony to safer havens. For their part the current Chinese leaders are mooting the creation of a huge economic zone in southern China, designed to strengthen links with the two enclaves to China's advantage but without bringing Hong Kong and Macao directly into the Chinese economic system. Under this scenario, economically advanced and large industrial cities would be used to help develop poor provinces on the periphery. In time the CCP may well tighten conditions regarding joint ventures, but some Hong Kong entrepreneurs may still be willing to co-operate if returns on investment are guaranteed.

Although such Chinese economic plans must surely be tentative, Japan's sizeable financial stake in Hong Kong,

Macao and Taiwan suggests that Japanese businessmen, whether on their own account or through the medium of overseas Chinese subsidiaries, will play an increasing role in China's modernization programme via compensation trade, joint ventures and Special Economic Zones.[19]

As economic co-operation between the two countries evolves, so will there be changes in the volume and commodity structure of Sino–Japanese trade. Before discussing the present and future direction of that market, however, a cursory examination of post-1949 Sino–Japanese trading relations is in order.

In the years immediately after their accession to power in 1949 the CCP leaders sought to eliminate all vestiges of earlier Japanese colonialism and assert themselves as representatives of an independent sovereign nation founded on socialist principles. With China a member of the international Communist movement, they wished to woo Japan away from the United States alliance and, stressing the subordination of economics to politics in foreign relations, attempted to use trade as a lever to obtain Japanese government recognition of their regime. Until the Sino–Japanese *rapprochement* in the early 1970s, however, the situation was not an easy one for the Japanese, allied as they were with the United States, and during the 1950s Sino–Japanese commerce could be conducted only through the face-saving device of unofficial informal trade on the barter principle. Initially, two-way trade was minimal, amounting to barely 60 million US dollars in 1950 and involving, for example, exchanges of Chinese coal and soybeans for Japanese textile machinery and galvanized iron plates. The United States strategic embargo on trade with Communist countries was partly responsible for the low level of activity, and in the late 1950s trade was virtually curtailed altogether because of increasingly stringent Chinese political conditions. Nevertheless China's Premier, Zhou Enlai, reopened trade in minor food and medical products in 1959 but simultaneously tried to exert political leverage, holding out the bait of further commerce.

It was not, however, until the early 1960s and the worsening of the Sino–Soviet dispute that the Chinese were prepared to make further concessions, no doubt with a long-term view of obtaining industrial equipment no longer being supplied by the Eastern bloc. Trade was still private and unofficial, with a monopoly created for the so-called friendly firms which operated through the mediation of Japanese Communist front organizations. Unfortunately, these companies were small operators unable to satisfy China's need for industrial plant, heavy machinery and fertilizers. By the early 1960s trade was being placed on a firmer footing; purchases were being paid for in cash and the Chinese dealt directly with Japanese manufacturers. In 1962 the semi-governmental Liao-Takasaki Agreement, named after the respective signatories, was signed. The friendly companies, however, continued to play a role. Trade continued to expand until the Cultural Revolution in 1966. The range of permissible goods was extended in 1967 with the institution of Memorandum Trade, which super-seded the 1962 accord and was renegotiated each year. Nevertheless, by the 1970s the Chinese were putting further pressure on Japan by refusing to do business with firms assisting the Taiwan economy or helping the American war effort in Vietnam.

During the 1960s Japanese companies, especially steel concerns, began to envisage a potentially lucrative China market and started to lobby sympathetic factional leaders in Japan's ruling Liberal Democratic Party (LDP). There were also pressures from other establishment circles, with LDP parliamentarians actively promoting the idea of diplomatic relations with the Chinese People's Republic. In addition, Japan's Ministry of International Trade and Industry (MITI), by virtue of its function, stood for increased trade with China, often in the teeth of opposition from the Foreign Office.

As a result of these developments and changes in the international situation, the value of Sino–Japanese trade increased, reaching a total of US$822 million in 1970, and Japan was already China's primary trading partner, account-ing for 20 per cent of her world total.[20] Moreover, when the Japanese Prime Minister, Tanaka, restored diplomatic rela-tions with China, severing official connections with the Chinese Nationalists on Taiwan, trade soared still more, as all

Japanese were now free to participate in China trade. Significantly, the Japanese imported Chinese crude oil for the first time in 1973 and Japan's government sought to boost trade by allowing the Chinese greater access to Export-Import Bank funding for industrial plant contracts.

In recent years the Japanese have been mounting a well-coordinated intelligence campaign to gain ascendancy over other Western countries in the Chinese market. Study of China's history and culture have long been included in the curricula of Japanese schools, and trading companies have established representative offices in Beijing, staffed by experienced Chinese-speaking employees. Such companies are additionally kept abreast of developments in China by the commercial attachés of the Embassy in Beijing. Japanese success is indicated by the fact that when Tanaka signed the normalization treaty in 1972, trade with China was worth US$1000 million a year; in 1982 its value was ten times greater.[21]

The commodity structure of Sino–Japanese trade necessarily reflects the economic priorities of the CCP. The Chinese are selling energy resources in order to purchase Japanese technology; exports of oil and coal currently loom large. For example, the Chinese contracted to supply Japan with two million tons of coking coal, mainly destined for the steel industry, in 1983; this was a considerable increase on the million or so tons shipped in 1980.[22] China, however, is not Japan's only source of supply, and in an era of low economic growth her buyers can afford to be selective. The quality of the Chinese product also varies, as control systems of local mines are distinctly inferior to those of state ones; in response to recent Japanese protests, however, the CCP leadership have promised to reconsider the ratios sold from each.

A similar logic applies to oil, in spite of considerable increases in Chinese oil exports during the 1970s and 1980s, with the Japanese buying a million tons in 1973 but eight million tons in 1980.[23] In the long run such sales are likely to help China pay for imports from Japan, but there are nevertheless several constraints in the short term. Chinese oil is low in sulphur but high in wax, causing difficulties in refining. In addition, Japan still has alternative sources, however vulnerable to disruption these may appear, and imports from China accounted for only about 3 per cent of Japan's total oil purchases in 1980. Finally, China has been growing too dependent on the Japanese market, which takes three-quarters of China's crude oil exports, as witnessed by China's acceptance in 1983 of a 15 per cent reduction in price. The Japanese were now paying US$28.70 per barrel, whereas a few years before they had paid US$37 for the same oil. This reflected, of course, a world glut.[24]

If Japanese technology and investment have boosted China's energy exports, improved telecommunications supplied with equipment from Japan will ultimately benefit China's economy as a whole. In 1981, for instance, Fujitsu Limited of Tokyo received an order for an electric telephone exchange system for Fujian, and in the same year computer-controlled automatic telecommunication relay equipment imported from Japan was installed in Canton, making possible the handling of 5400 telegrams an hour.

To date the CCP's readjustment policies have stressed light industry as opposed to heavy industry but even though the import of complete plant from Japan has been accordingly reduced during the early 1980s, purchases of steel have remained necessary for the manufacture of consumer goods. In addition, there are already signs that heavy industry is receiving renewed emphasis. In late 1982, for instance, China negotiated with Japan a loan to be used for the petrochemical and iron and steel industries.[25] Earlier, the Chinese had placed an additional order with Japanese steel-makers for shipment of 112,000 tons of ordinary steel products during the first half of the same year.[26]

Promotion of consumer goods industries has led to increased imports from Japan of production lines, like that installed in early 1981 at the Beijing Television Factory. This has a daily output capacity of 500 14-inch and 20-inch sets.[27] Unlike most television sets, which will be sold on the domestic market as part of the policy to give incentives to China's workforce, other consumer goods – such as textiles – are often destined for export, especially to Japan. China still has a strong competitive edge in natural fibre and textile products, including carpets and tablecloths, sectors which rely heavily on traditional technology. Some modern textile plant, however, has been imported from Japan since the mid-1960s. In 1980 the Chinese gained a 40 per cent share of Japan's cotton fabric imports, even forcing competitors from Taiwan and Hong Kong out of the market, and China's man-made fibres were equally successful.[28] These successes at least partially reflect China's being granted preferential tariff treatment for its exports to Japan in 1980, a decision taken by Japan's government in the hope that further industrialization and economic development in China would in turn stimulate demand for a wide range of Japanese goods.

The health of China's economy, however, still depends on agriculture to feed a growing population and as far as possible obviate the necessity of spending precious foreign exchange on grain imports. To increase yields, greater fertilizer application is crucial, especially because the land has been overworked throughout the centuries. China is Japan's largest market for such chemical products as ammonium sulphate and urea, while large plants using Japanese technology and equipment have been installed to produce synthetic fertilizers.[29]

With this perspective of Sino-Japanese trade since 1949 we are now in a position to evaluate its importance to each country and suggest possible future trends. In 1981 Japan was China's foremost trading partner, with two-way trade reaching US$10,000 million; a year earlier the Sino–Japanese relationship accounted for almost a quarter of China's total world trade and China had become the fourth biggest market for Japanese goods. These trends have continued, even if bilateral trade fell slightly in 1982, being valued at almost nine billion US dollars. In the same year steel and steel products accounted for 36.8 per cent of total Japanese exports to China. The high proportion of mining and agricultural machinery undoubtedly reflected economic readjustment priorities, but increased Chinese purchases of galvanized plates pointed to growth in heavy industry and a strong demand for electrical applicances as well as other consumer goods. In exchange, Japan imported crude oil, coal and textile products.[30]

One conspicuous trend in these years was a trade balance in

China's favour. In 1982 Japanese exports to China declined sharply by 31.1 per cent from the previous year to US$3511 million, while imports increased by 1.1 per cent over the same period to stand at US$5352 million, resulting in a US$1841 million deficit for Japan, the second in a row.[31] Certainly, the Chinese leaders continue to see Japan as a major export market but are careful not to rely too heavily on one country as a major source of much-needed technology and equipment.

In extending the 1978 Japan–China Long Term Trade Agreement, Chinese and Japanese negotiators have expressed the intention of increasing export volume and value well into the 1990s. While it would be simplistic to suggest that the two economies are complementary, current trends would seem to indicate that the Chinese will concentrate on imports of key equipment which cannot be manufactured domestically, but yet is crucial for the exploitation of China's natural resources, like oil and coal. These, in turn, will be exported to meet the needs of Japanese energy-consuming industries. In conclusion, in spite of the two countries' respective commitments elsewhere, the Sino–Japanese trading relationship is likely to assume even greater significance in the decades to come. The political ramifications of Sino–Japanese economic co-operation in the wider context of Asia and the world will be one of the themes of our concluding chapter.

5 Conclusions:
Towards a Sino–Japanese Axis

A consistent theme in Chinese foreign policy since the Communist accession, in spite of divisions on other issues within the leadership, has been support for armed revolution in the economically developing areas of Asia, Africa and Latin America, and, where such movements have been successful, the Chinese leaders encourage governments of the new states to eliminate any vestiges of influence exerted by the old colonial powers. Thus the Chinese see their revolution as a model to be emulated by Third World nationalist leaders both in the struggle to gain power, through guerrilla strategy, and as a method of economic development, via policies of self-reliance and internal generation of capital without benefit of external aid. But even though the Chinese leaders train guerrilla fighters from such areas, proffer limited economic assistance and despatch technical advisers, their major commitment to revolution has been a moral one and China claims to adhere to the dictum that revolution cannot be exported.

By the early 1970s the Chinese perceived that the constellation of forces in the world balance of power was shifting; the Soviet leaders who had earlier exacted a heavy price for the loans afforded to China during the 1950s were now portrayed as social imperialists who had betrayed the cause of world revolution, especially in the developing areas of Asia, Africa and Latin America. Moreover, the Chinese believed that the Soviet Union had a stake in the current economic and political *status quo*; its leadership were therefore unwilling to sacrifice national interests for the cause of revolution in the Third World. Furthermore, as the Sino–Soviet dispute had intensified during the late 1960s, Russian troop concentrations on the border posed a growing security threat to China but the United States, having recently withdrawn from Vietnam, appeared as the weaker of the two superpowers.

The Chinese response to these changes was given coherent formulation in Mao Zedong's 'three zones' theory; identification was still with the Third World but limited collaboration was now possible with the advanced industrial countries of the 'second zone', for example the states of the EEC and Japan, and even with the less dangerous superpower, the United States.

The kind of simplistic framework within which the Chinese leaders, until recently, so often conducted their foreign policy was in part at least a legacy of China's initial abrupt introduction to a Western-dominated system of international relations in the mid-nineteenth century. In spite of military and diplomatic reversals at the hands of Western colonial powers, successive Chinese governments, although of differing political complexions, continued to consider China the 'Middle Kingdom', the centre of civilisation, and this had far-reaching implications for both the formulation and conduct of China's foreign policy. Marxism-Leninism, a foreign ideology, was given a uniquely Chinese cast; China's moral superiority was assumed and propagated to the world, informing all her pronouncements on international affairs. Thus her leaders were confident that, through force of example, her new civilization would naturally be followed, especially by the new states. Nevertheless, in the day-to-day conduct of foreign relations Chinese leaders had to take account of conflicts and divisions among the nations; just as, in the face of the struggle between colonial powers for concessions in China, Chinese rulers sought 'to use barbarians to control barbarians' by playing off one European country against another, so were the United States and her allies seen collectively as a counterweight to Soviet might during the late 1960s and early 1970s. Such simple formulas, however, have not always served the Chinese leaders well, and appear even less likely to do so in the future.

Although, for example, the current Chinese leaders remain ultimately committed to world revolution as sanctioned by

Marxist-Leninist doctrine, and share such Third World economic concerns as better terms of trade for primary produce and raw materials – as expressed, for instance, at United Nations forums – there are now areas of divergence between Chinese interests and those of other developing countries. Furthermore, one stimulus to China's *rapprochement* with the West during the early 1970s was that there were limits to economic self-reliance, and future Chinese development would depend on the acquisition of technology and investment available from the United States, Europe and Japan, but not the Third World.

Against this background the Chinese leaders have recently shown signs of rejecting the old stark categories of friends and enemies. Apprehensive as ever concerning the danger of foreigners controlling China's economy, they give top priority to national security in its widest sense, and an ambitious modernization programme, itself demanding a stable international environment, is increasingly seen as the best guarantee of defence. It was in this spirit that Premier Zhao Ziyang outlined his country's new foreign policy stance at the Sixth National People's Congress held in June 1983. The substance of Zhao's message and later Chinese policy statements may well reflect the growing complexity of international affairs; issues relating, for instance, to China's growing participation in world trade and economic relations with Western powers are no longer amenable to simple definition in terms of the major enemy theory. China's leaders now consider international relations from a 'multidimensional' rather than a 'unidimensional' perspective, and concrete examples will serve to illustrate their new multilateral and issue-oriented foreign policy.[1]

On a visit to the United States in January 1984 Zhao Ziyang reiterated China's fundamental principles of safeguarding world peace, promoting international justice, and defending the basic rights and interests of peoples everywhere, especially the Chinese and the Third World. The five conditions of mutual respect, mutual accommodation, equality, mutual benefit and peaceful co-existence would serve as the foundation of relations between countries with different social systems; all countries should pledge to act according to universally acknowledged norms governing international intercourse, instead of trying to impose the laws and systems of one on the other. Thus the Chinese could never compromise on the question of Taiwan and any sales of arms to the Nationalist government on the island were tantamount to interference in China's internal affairs. But this dispute, as well as the need to criticize the United States on a number of international issues – especially in relation to the Third World – need not preclude common cause on other world problems or the more immediate question of economic co-operation between the two countries. The Chinese leaders would thus never reverse their policy of an economic open door to the outside world, and Zhao was at pains to reassure foreign investors of preferential treatment and guaranteed profits at minimal risk. Financial arrangements would facilitate closer political ties, and the modernization programme offer further pecuniary advantage to both sides.

The Chinese are now conducting relations with the Soviet Union on similar principles. In the foreseeable future a return to the Sino–Soviet alliance of the 1950s is out of the question, and in any case China's current foreign policy stance would seem to rule it out. But even Soviet refusal to accommodate Chinese demands concerning the occupation of Afghanistan, support of Vietnamese ambitions in Southeast Asia, and troop concentrations on the Sino–Soviet border have not been barriers to recent economic agreements between the two major Communist powers. Thus, although the Soviet Union remains the main ostensible military threat to China, bilateral trade increased substantially in 1983 and a new student exchange scheme has been initiated. In fact, Soviet expertise could yet prove invaluable in certain sectors of China's modernization programme, especially as many industrial enterprises were originally constructed according to Soviet blueprints during the period of the First Five-Year Plan (1953–7), and much may be learned from the experience of Russia, a country with a similar social system and command economy. The two countries, then, have certain interests in common, in spite of the Chinese leaders' opposition to what they see as the Soviet superpower's attempt to extend its sphere of influence worldwide, especially in Southeast Asia, at the expense not only of the United States, Third and second world countries but, more importantly, China's own national security.

Thus, even though China's foreign policy is increasingly issue-oriented, the categories of the 'three zones' are retained as a tool of analysis, and the Chinese leadership still place faith in the second world as a counterweight to the two superpowers.

Although there are fewer contentious issues in China's relations with Japan, the Chinese leadership do not necessarily subscribe to all aspects of Japanese defence and foreign policy. Bilateral consultations between ministers of the two governments have brought consensus on a number of political and economic issues, but the Chinese are apprehensive concerning apparent Japanese willingness to undertake an increased defence role in the region at the behest of the United States. While China's leaders are in favour of the 'moral' rather than the strictly legal interpretation of Article 9, the 'peace clause' in the 1947 Japanese Constitution, and therefore support the view that Japan, in common with all other states, has the inherent right of self-defence, they have nevertheless expressed serious concern over a possible militarist revival in that country. The defence of Japan itself, especially in the face of increased Soviet power, is acceptable to the Chinese; but a greater independent Japanese military role in the region would be viewed with suspicion.

Just as the Chinese leaders see modernization as a prerequisite for national defence, so also have the Japanese posited their participation in bilateral and multilateral aid programmes on the assumption that improved living standards in Asian countries are in the best interests of political stability. As has been noted, Sino–Japanese trade largely reflects the complementary nature of the two economies, with Japan exporting such heavy industrial products as steel plants and machinery, and importing China's crude oil, coal, mineral products and raw materials. The ongoing Japanese contribution to China's development necessarily reflects the stage and pace of her economic strategy.

In the early 1980s an economic readjustment programme was introduced in China as previously there had been excess heavy industrial capacity, not all of which was efficient. More significantly, heavy industry drew off a disproportionate share of raw materials and energy from light industry, which now had the crucial task of producing consumer goods as incentives for the urban and rural workforce. Stress was also placed on the technical reform of existing enterprises involving improvement in basic processes, technical innovation, renewal of facilities and reconstruction of factories. It was clear, however, that once the period of consolidation was over production in heavy industry would have to increase to satisfy the needs of light industry and fuel further economic advance. But, on the negative side, as of early 1984 any excessive growth in the heavy industrial sector has also been due to poorly controlled spending at the provincial level, itself a reflection of the greater independence granted to local authorities. Such trends, then, were evident in 1983 but although growth in heavy industry reached 13 per cent, or well above the 3.9 per cent target, this did not hinder light industry, whose output increased by 8 per cent, almost twice the figure planned.[2]

Thus trade with Japan is necessarily related to the timetable of economic development. China, like other developing economies at an equivalent stage, is having to import large quantities of steel, domestic output of which cannot keep pace with growth in industrial production as a whole. Although the fourth largest steel producers in the world, the Chinese still purchase 20 per cent of the steel they need from abroad, especially from Japan.

In 1983 Sino–Japanese bilateral trade increased, reversing the 14.7 per cent fall of the previous year, and resulted in a Japanese trade deficit of only US\$173 million as opposed to an equivalent figure of US\$1841 million in 1982.

Expansion of Chinese imports was due to greater investment in basic construction and concomitant purchases of steel worth US\$2203.92 million. Japanese exports of machinery and equipment to China went up by 28 per cent to US\$1378.78 million.

Sino–Japanese bilateral trade 1983 (unit: US $million)

Japanese exports		Japanese imports		Total		Balance
Value	Increase over previous year	Value	Increase over previous year	Value	Increase over previous year	
4,914	40%	5,087	−5%	10,001	12.8%	−173

For some years Japan has been seeking supplies of oil alternative to those of the politically volatile Middle East, and exploitation of domestic energy resources has been one of China's major economic priorities. Oil and coal loomed large in Japan's imports from China in 1983, even though prices of these commodities actually fell. Significantly, in 1982 China had become the fifth largest crude oil supplier for Japan after Saudi Arabia, Indonesia, the United Arab Emirates and Iran. Although these purchases satisfied only a small percentage of Japan's needs in 1983, they accounted for 60 per cent of China's total oil exports. Moreover, production of Chinese crude oil increased by 3.8 per cent over 1982 and new oil reserves are now being discovered. In addition, in 1983 China was Japan's fifth largest source of coal after Australia, the United States, Canada and South Africa. Once again, these sales were important to China as they represented nearly half her total coal exports.[3] Finally, by the early 1980s a third of Chinese imports came from Japan, which in turn was taking 20 per cent of China's exports; even more importantly, Sino–Japanese trade accounted for over half of China's total trade with Western industrial countries.

Hu Yaobang, General Secretary of the CCP, has proposed that the two countries aim to quadruple bilateral trade by the end of the century, and this must be seen within the wider context of economic co-operation. China's new long-term economic development programme, adopted in September 1982, called for a fourfold increase in agricultural and industrial production by the year 2000. One key product is steel, output of which is scheduled to double during the same period. While the Chinese have recently been discussing with the

Soviet leaders the possibility of assistance in modernizing the major plants built and equipped with Russian aid in the 1950s, improvement of existing steelworks can be only a partial solution to the problem of increasing production capacity. More pertinent is the Chinese decision to construct steelworks modelled on Japan's most advanced factories, incorporating such features as controlled automation of the processing system. One example of Sino–Japanese co-operation is the Shanghai Baoshan Steel Complex, the development of which was halted in the wake of readjustment but is now once again in progress. Not only will the plant provide a crucial material for the overall benefit of the surrounding Yangtze River Delta area but its modern technology and equipment will make it a pace-setter in the modernization of China's economy as a whole.

While projects like the Baoshan Complex have meant extensive government involvement on both sides, Japanese business is expressing increasing interest in undertaking joint ventures with Chinese concerns. A survey conducted by the Industrial Bank of Japan elicited a positive response from 57.2 per cent of over 800 firms operating in a wide range of industries. Such links would, it was argued, offer major advantages: the great potential of the Chinese market, a cheap and abundant labour force, and rich raw material resources. Economically advanced regions like Shanghai, Beijing, and Guangdong-Fujian were preferred, especially because of better physical infrastructure and concentration of technical expertise.[4]

To date, however, Japanese joint venture investment has been low in proportion to the total, even though Japan is China's foremost trading partner. Official Chinese sources may nevertheless underestimate the extent of Japanese participation since – as suggested earlier – Hong Kong undertakings, themselves in some cases subsidiaries of Japanese companies, have a sizeable stake in joint ventures. But there are, in any case, obstacles to further Japanese involvement: in spite of declared commitment to a form of market socialism and at least partial adherence to the profit motive, the Chinese retain a command economy, unlike Japan's free enterprise.

Japanese businessmen are yet to be entirely convinced of China's political stability and economic direction, fearing that reforms to date may be reversed in the event of leadership changes, despite attempts at reassurance by China's elder statesman, Deng Xiaoping, and his supporters. To allay disquiet, further inducements have recently been offered to foreign investors: it was announced in January 1984 that, in future, joint venture enterprises would be permitted to sell part of their output on the Chinese domestic market instead of having to produce exclusively for export. In addition advanced machinery and equipment, unavailable in China and imported by joint ventures, have been exempt from Chinese import duties, as well as industrial and commercial consolidated tax, since the beginning of February 1984. This rule applies to ventures in most economic sectors.[5]

But Japanese firms nevertheless have serious reservations about the health and effectiveness of China's economic system. Thus, although China's individual enterprises and local authorities have been given greater autonomy, with profitability the stated criterion of efficiency, ingrained bureaucratic habits die hard. Chinese managers still display reluctance to take personal initiative, fearing a possible change of heart on the part of the nation's top leadership. Japan's senior enterprise management, in contrast, has a tradition of decision-making through general consensus, after considering free market factors and the interests of the company as a whole. Thus there are signs that Chinese middle managers and administrators have still not fully grasped the attitudes necessary to achieve competitiveness on both domestic and foreign markets.

Nevertheless, by virtue of a cultural heritage shared with the Chinese, the Japanese are better placed than the developing countries to help impart the values, the philosophical infrastructure, indispensable for the success of China's modernization programme.

The economic complementarity of China and Japan has often been emphasized but much less weight has been given to how the long cultural association between the two countries may help the Chinese to preserve their national integrity in the midst of increasing trade and economic co-operation with Western powers, and at the same time aid Japan's quest for a more positive national identity.

From 1868 onwards the Meiji leaders, building on traditional social structures and values, were able to develop political institutions and an economic system which satisfied the aspirations of the Japanese people, thereby promoting modernization and preserving national sovereignty until defeat in war in 1945.

Japan's identity, however, has been much less secure; economically, she has surpassed most Western countries on their own terms but historically and culturally she is indubitably part of Asia. Japan's pre-war militarists conceived of a divine mission to draw Asian people out of backwardness towards modernity and eradicate Western influence from the continent, through both military conquest and economic hegemony; in post-war decades, in contrast, the Japanese have participated in bilateral and multilateral aid programmes to Asian countries but are only just beginning to formulate a positive independent foreign policy beyond purely economic concerns. In this sense the Japanese may be seen as a nation still in search of an identity because they have failed to integrate aspects of a culture largely derivative from both Chinese and Western sources. If China may make good Japan's deficiency in raw materials, it is by analogy not too fanciful to suggest that greater understanding between the two countries in all spheres of endeavour could give the Japanese a more confident national identity by their returning to the major source of their culture, without posing a serious threat to other Asian states.

The Chinese, however, even in the wake of infringement of sovereignty and economic collapse occasioned by invasion and war, remained firm believers in the superiority of their culture and civilization. But the leadership's economic open door policy, seen as crucial for their modernization programme, entails a risk to the viability of China's less secure authority structures. Greater exposure to Western media, especially advertising of consumer goods on Hong Kong television – now received by millions in Southern China – is already creating rising expectations among the population at large. In addition, increased contact with foreign business is leading to venality among officials. A third danger is to Chinese civilization itself were, for example, Western art and literary forms adopted to the exclusion of traditional models, with a resulting decline in the vitality of China's own culture.

It could equally well be argued, however, that newly evolving institutions, especially those informed by the profit motive, will naturally leave their mark on social values and benefit the national economy; and there is no reason why Chinese culture should not be enriched by contact with the West. On a visit to Canada in January 1984 Premier Zhao Ziyang stated that his country welcomed Western technology, education, and culture but failed to outline criteria of acceptability, except in the most general terms. The Chinese leaders are nevertheless apprehensive lest such developments produce short-term instability and threaten their own personal positions. But the solution to all these problems, called 'capitalist erosion' or 'cultural pollution' by the Chinese, may well be facilitated by the extensive formal apparatus of security control characteristic of a Marxist-Leninist political and social system. Additionally, Deng Xiaoping and his supporters have been calling for 'class struggle' between the forces of capitalism and socialism, with emphasis on patriotic education – particularly among youth – seen as a powerful weapon against potentially undesirable foreign influences.

Whenever the Chinese leaders consider foreign economic activity suspect, charges of 'capitalist erosion' can just as well be directed against Japan as other Western powers. There is a sense, however, in which the Japanese are in a unique position to act as 'cultural mediators' between China and the West. Since 1868 the Japanese have been adopting Western institutions and technology while preserving their own cultural heritage; in fact, the survival of traditional social values has fostered the kind of discipline necessary for sustained economic growth. In both Chinese and Japanese societies there has been a long tradition of subordinating the individual to the group, and there seems no reason why the collective ethic in China cannot in future be harnessed to create new forms of

social solidarity more in keeping with the current modernization programme.

Certainly, Japan's social values and structures cannot be
directly transplanted to China, but lessons may nevertheless
be learned from Japanese successes in such areas as man-
agement-labour relations, especially in view of growing
Japanese participation in joint ventures. Chinese industrial
enterprises still operate within the confines of a command
economy but are now closer in function to their Western and
Japanese counterparts, and no longer do they merely need to
fulfil, as in the past, the low targets set by the state. Greater
autonomy granted to enterprises in management and decision-making, together with material incentives for the workforce to increase output, are intended to achieve greater
efficiency and maximize profits. Japanese industrial management has long been known for its paternalism which, of
course, works two ways: in exchange for unswerving loyalty
and hard work, employees receive permanent tenure of
employment as well as extensive provision of health, welfare
and leisure amenities in addition to salary. Thus while recent
Chinese reforms may well succeed in injecting a healthy blast
of competitiveness into the economy, traditional Chinese
collective loyalties, if in future centred on individual industrial
concerns, could at the same time act in conjunction with
effective bonus schemes to push forward the country's modernization programme. In this context the Chinese may gain
from Japanese experience in promoting industrial efficiency
and barring unacceptable aspects of Western culture.

Thus only through wider cultural co-operation will greater
understanding and mutual trust between the Chinese and
Japanese peoples be fostered, to the long-term benefit of both
parties. In addition to intensified ministerial level consultations on a broad range of issues, the current generation of
leaders are now actively promoting further exchanges between
various sectors of the two societies, especially youth.

A case in point was the decision to establish the 21st
Century Committee, taken during CCP General Secretary Hu
Yao-bang's visit to Japan in 1983. The Committee, to be
composed of representatives of old, middle-aged and young

scholars, economists and politicians, is designed to sow the seeds of mutual trust between future generations.

There are, however, considerable obstacles to genuine unfettered cultural exchanges, particularly in the media. The West, including Japan, tends to cast intellectuals, artists, and the media as society's critics; in China they have traditionally been seen as servants of a ruling orthodoxy. In mid-1981 a CCP periodical attacked a Japanese mass-media report alleging increasing social division in China and took particular exception to suggestions of discord within China's leadership and references to economic difficulties. Such criticism of government performance, whether at home or abroad, is naturally considered the very stuff of journalistic reporting in Japan. Exchanges of, for instance, television personnel will nevertheless bring technical improvement for both sides and perhaps ultimately help the Chinese to accept the need for more critical comment in their media as a whole.

In addition to cultural exchanges there is also co-operation in the more narrowly defined field of education. A premium is now being placed on specialist knowledge, as the CCP's credibility will increasingly rest on the nation's economic performance. While Mao Zedong was alive mass campaigns, which reached their zenith in the Cultural Revolution (1966–9), placed political commitment higher than technical expertise, and anti-intellectual attitudes, whether among certain Party members or some sections of the general population, die hard. It will thus be the task of the education system not only to impart knowledge but to inculcate those attitudes which will facilitate the optimum use of technological competence.

The introduction of expertise from abroad, in say the cybernetics field, will eventually render China's employment system more complex, create diverse centres of economic power, and allow new technocratic élites to emerge. If social dissidence is to be kept to a minimum and rising expectations satisfied, the population as a whole must be educated to accept these new patterns of social status as legitimate.

Post-war Japan may be considered a meritocracy, with academic performance the major determinant of social mobility, and she shares with China Confucian assumptions concerning the nature of man and knowledge, one prominent feature of which is stress on determined sustained effort rather than innate ability as the key factor in learning. Thus man is by nature good, the implication being that all are capable of becoming experts or rulers. The CCP leaders have also inherited this legacy and access to education, especially the universities, is now based on fiercely competitive entry examinations.

The Chinese have closely examined the Japanese education system and sent students for training in Japan itself. In 1981 Japan signed an agreement granting China 50 million yen to be spent on education and research. This has not, however, guaranteed that the latest knowledge is properly utilized in Chinese industry and commerce. Vested interests in China's economic establishment have resisted change; young bankers, for example, despatched overseas to acquire the latest expertise, have not been given free rein to institute reforms in the banking system on their return to China due to obstruction by top leaders in the banks. The need for professional competence in Chinese industry must be readily acknowledged; in January 1984 a Chinese press source admitted that business accounting and management in some enterprises had been deficient, resulting in serious wastage of resources.

There are problems, too, in the legal field. Conclusion of contracts, for instance in the case of joint ventures, has often been delayed because Chinese lawyers, who act as advisers, are not well versed in Chinese laws. In addition Chinese laws themselves often leave much to be desired, and must be improved if investors from abroad are to be reassured concerning the safety of their financial stake. In this field there has also been consultation with the Japanese.

In fact, of all the Western powers the Japanese are perhaps in the best position to inculcate a professional ethic, without which stress on market forces and profits will be inadequate to sustain long-term economic growth.[6]

At present Sino–Japanese relations rest mainly on economic co-operation, but greater co-ordination of the two countries' domestic policies will ultimately have repercussions in the field of foreign affairs and intergovernmental consultation, ever since the first such meeting in December 1980, has placed international as well as domestic issues on the agenda. On regaining their sovereignty in 1952 after the American Occupation the Japanese, mindful of their country's few national resources, began to conduct omnidirectional diplomacy. At the beginning of the Cold War in the late 1940s the Americans stressed the rehabilitation of Japan's economy and helped to introduce the Japanese to world markets. Aware that their country possessed few natural resources, Japan's leaders staked their country's standard of living on competitive exports and, reluctant to offend potential customers and suppliers, sought amicable relations with all countries. This economic foreign policy paid dividends while the world's raw materials and energy supplies remained abundant, but became less workable with oil price increases in the 1970s and an increasingly politically volatile Middle East by the 1980s.

In addition Japan has sheltered under the American nuclear umbrella, long assuming that any full-scale attack on the Japanese islands would activate the Defence Treaty with the United States. Meanwhile, however, by the 1970s there was growing feeling in the Western alliance that the American relationship helped the Japanese to avoid substantial increases in defence expenditure, leaving Japan's budget free for more aggressive commercial expansion at home and abroad. Recent United States administrations have been pressing Japan to shoulder a greater defence burden, a policy now also increasingly advocated by a growing section of informed Japanese public opinion and government leaders, especially in the wake of an intensified Soviet naval build-up in the Pacific and doubts about American commitment to protect Japan in the event of war.

As discussed earlier, until the 1980s Japanese policy-makers tended to see their country's defence and the political stability of the Asian region as a whole in terms of economic development. Particularly since Nakasone's election as Prime Minister, however, such thinking has undergone a change, with calls for a more positive foreign policy which seeks to influence rather than react to international events. Contributions to the material welfare of the world community through aid and trade remain a pivot of Japanese defence; but military capacity, ostensibly to be developed on the basis of Japan's own resources, is now being given greater priority than at any time during the post-war period.

The Japanese, the only people in the world to suffer attack by atomic weapons, have suffered a 'nuclear allergy', and Prime Minister Nakasone built on these sentiments when, at the opening of the new Diet session in February 1984, he called upon the two superpowers, the United States and the Soviet Union, to negotiate reductions in nuclear armaments and ultimately eliminate them from the life of mankind. He emphasized that only a country like Japan, without such an arsenal and with only a defensive military capability, could argue persuasively for peace and disarmament. In fact, it was the United States which in 1946 imposed upon Japan a new democratic constitution, Article 9 of which renounced war as a sovereign right of the Japanese nation, denying entitlement to maintain land, sea and air forces. The intention, of course, was to prevent the revival of Japanese militarism. Aware, however, of Japan's potential as an ally against Communism in Asia, the Americans subsequently encouraged conservative Japanese governments to develop a paramilitary police reserve, later transformed into the Self-Defence Forces. Article 9 was accordingly given a moral interpretation rather than a strictly legal one. Japan, in common with other nations, was said to enjoy the inalienable right of self-defence. Substantial increases in military manpower and equipment have thus been possible without constitutional amendment, which would have required a concurring vote of two-thirds or more of all members in each House of the Japanese Diet, with subsequent ratification by an affirmative majority at a popular referendum. But a government decision to develop nuclear weapons would be a different question.

Japan's defence, then, is still seen in terms of conventional forces operating within the framework of the United States alliance. In 1983 the Defence Agency of Japan called for close co-operation with the West to counter the Soviet military build-up in Asia, and for the first time in a White Paper referred to protection of Japanese sea lanes. Consequently, the nation's defence is being strengthened to guarantee lines of communication within a radius of several hundred miles and, in the event of an armed attack on Japan, to protect sea routes for about 1000 nautical miles. Some private sources have nevertheless cast doubts on the credibility of Japan's national defence, warning that budgetary allocations are insufficient even for the 1983–7 military build-up plan, let alone any wider commitments in the Asian region. Japan is, of course, vulnerable to economic blockade; the bulk of her oil from the Middle East, for instance, passes through the narrow Straits of Malacca. Current expenditure is, however, intended strictly for defence of the Japanese islands rather than in relation to any broader responsibilities, such as those the United States seems to advocate for Japan as a member of the Western alliance.[7]

Chinese attitudes to post-war Japanese rearmament have undergone considerable change. During the 1950s and 1960s the Party-controlled press in China continually warned against the revival of Japanese militarism under United States auspices, and only with Mao Zedong's reformulation of foreign policy in the early 1970s did the leadership move cautiously towards acceptance of a greater role for Japan in the security of Asia, albeit within the framework of the United States alliance. The Americans would thus guarantee Japanese good behaviour. By the early 1980s discreet Sino –Japanese military consultations at a high level were taking place in the wake of increased economic co-operation; greater priority given to defence expenditure by the Japanese government being considered in the Chinese view a crucial counterweight to Soviet power in the region. This latter view has now been qualified since the formulation of an issue-oriented policy on the part of the Chinese. They support the Japanese leaders' right to maintain Self-Defence Forces and share apprehension concerning Soviet activity, but the possibility of any formal Sino–Japanese military alliance must be ruled out unless there is a radical change in the Asian balance of power.

The leaders of China and Japan have pledged themselves to work towards international disarmament but both have implied that the major initiative in reducing nuclear and conventional forces must rest with the superpowers. Although the Chinese have publicly abjured participation in the arms race, giving priority instead to economic construction and improvement of the people's livelihood, they possess nuclear weapons and have refused to sign the Nuclear Non-Proliferation Treaty on the grounds that it reinforces superpower supremacy. The Japanese did sign the Treaty and have long been developing nuclear energy for peaceful purposes.

Even given future Japanese willingness to develop nuclear weapons, China and Japan, whether singly or in co-operation, would take many decades to match the arsenals of the superpowers. Any Sino–Japanese military collaboration is thus likely to be defensive rather than offensive and designed primarily to maintain the power balance in Asia. In January 1984 Premier Zhao Ziyang stressed that the Chinese would rely mainly on their own efforts to modernize defence capacity. This does not, however, preclude regular consultation and exchange of personnel with second world countries like Japan, and Chinese purchases of military technology. In addition, other forms of technical co-operation could serve to enhance war potential. At government level talks with the Japanese, held in Beijing in December 1983, the Chinese agreed in principle on the early conclusion of an accord on importing nuclear technology exclusively for peaceful purposes. The two countries are also pursuing the possibility of jointly developing China's uranium resources and conducting research into the processing of used radioactive materials. Japanese knowhow will no doubt be invaluable in the construction of the nuclear power stations in East and Northeast China now being planned. But – in accordance with their commitment to the terms of the Non-Proliferation Treaty – the Japanese seek safeguards against the military use of such knowledge, especially as some sources suggest that the Chinese have in the past exported information concerning nuclear power to other countries.

In early 1984 reports of evidence presented to the United States Congress indicated that the Chinese had transferred sensitive nuclear weapons design information to Pakistan, even though the leaders of that country have in the past denied any interest in manufacturing a nuclear bomb.

The Chinese will not in any case rely exclusively on Japan for military equipment or technology, as they are at times suspicious of Japanese motives. Moreover, the Japanese have often shown themselves insensitive to Chinese feelings, for example during the 1982 controversy over revised Japanese history textbooks which referred to Japan's wartime invasion of China as an 'advance' instead of aggression and glossed over atrocities committed by Japan during the years from 1937 to 1945. Nor were the Chinese reassured by subsequent Japanese Education Ministry claims that amendments were the responsibility of publishers, not the government.

The two countries nevertheless make common cause on certain international questions, and it is clear that in the years to come no major Asian issue will be solved without consultation with both these powers. A case in point is Korea, where the government in Pyongyang is pledged to reunify the peninsula on Communist terms. In January 1984 it was revealed that Japan had joined the United States, China and South Korea in a series of secret consultations, held the previous autumn, to bring about peace talks with North Korea and achieve a measure of stability in North Asia.[8] Both China and Japan would have much to lose by a unified Communist Korea; the Chinese fear the pro-Soviet orientation of the Pyongyang regime and the Japanese are apprehensive concerning their country's own national security.

This common concern with Soviet expansionism extends to other parts of the region. A number of nations in Southeast Asia traditionally fell within China's cultural orbit, and although generally never subject to direct Chinese rule were nevertheless considered tributary states by China's earlier dynastic rulers. The Chinese Communists have certainly sought to extend their influence, aiming at least at the creation of friendly buffer states on their country's southern borders. They undoubtedly seek to reverse the *status quo* in Kampuchea (formerly Cambodia) and thereby stem the tide of Soviet-backed Vietnamese power, a traditional rival in the region.

In spite of continuing commitment to world revolution,

however, the Chinese, barring a radical change of leadership, seem unlikely to undertake any major military adventures, because of both the breathing space needed for their ambitious modernization programme and the limited logistical capability of China's conventional forces outside her borders. Much of China's military equipment is in any case obsolete and needs to be replaced by extensive arms purchases abroad.

In the post-war period Japanese activity in the region has been economic. Japanese aid and investment – partly altruistic, partly self-interested – has been directed towards exploiting the rich natural resources of the region, with resulting imports fuelling Japan's hungry industries.

But perceived Chinese expansionism and Japan's war record make incumbent Southeast Asia élites wary of both countries' motives. Overseas Chinese in, say, Malaysia and Indonesia have often been seen as China's fifth column, and the leaders of Singapore, a state with a large Chinese majority, steer clear of too close an involvement with China. These states, however, are newly industrializing countries and they are compelled to acknowledge the potential influence which China and Japan could exert in the region. Their economic growth rates are singularly impressive but in the long term will be maintained only with massive infusions of Western technology, particularly via the already considerable Japanese investment and trade. China, on the other hand, has natural resources which could lead to greater trade with the countries of the area.

Suspicion of Japan is to some extent being mitigated by Japanese participation in multilateral, rather than bilateral, aid programmes under the auspices of such bodies as the United Nations and the Asian Development Bank. China's growing role in international organizations could also serve as a prelude to greater co-operation in regional development. While concerted Sino-Japanese economic or political initiatives would no doubt be viewed with apprehension in the region, the two countries individually could contribute much to general stability in Asia and such efforts might well be channelled through existing regional bodies or new arrangements. A balance would thereby be created, preventing any preponderant influence by either country.

Moreover, in January 1984 Zhao Ziyang reiterated China's view that Asia and the Pacific should be freed of superpower military bases and forces and implicitly stated the goal of creating an internal balance of power in the region. This idea is similar to the concept of a Pacific basin group of states, comprising Japan, the United States, China, Southeast Asia and Australasia and mooted recently in some Western ruling circles as an economic and strategic counterweight to Soviet power. The latter arrangement might meet with future Chinese approval, depending presumably on the nature of the American commitment. The Japanese, for their part, are in any case increasingly taking responsibility for their own defence and pursuing independent initiatives in international affairs, albeit as yet within the framework of the Western alliance. The twenty-first century could see a scenario of this kind and the emergence of a Sino-Japanese axis, a new civilization built on Chinese culture and Japanese technology, to the lasting benefit of the peoples of Asia.

Notes

1 Introduction: Contemporary trends

1 See Sadako Ogata, 'The business community and Japanese foreign policy: Normalization of relations with the People's Republic of China', in Robert A. Scalapino (ed.), *The Foreign Policy of Modern Japan* (Berkeley, California, 1977), pp.181–91.

2 This issue is discussed in Akio Watanabe, 'Japanese public opinion and foreign policy, 1964–1973', in Scalapino, pp.124–8.

3 For a development of this theme see Harry Harding, 'China and the Third World', in Richard Solomon, *The China Factor* (Englewood Cliffs, NJ, 1981), p.277.

4 *People's Daily*, 20 February 1982, in *Summary of World Broadcasts* (hereafter *SWB*), 22 February 1982.

5 The latter point is raised by Robert A. Scalapino, 'China and Northeast Asia', in Solomon, p.214.

6 Gerald Segal, 'China's strategic posture and the Great Power triangle', *Pacific Affairs*, 53, 4, Winter 1980–81, pp.682–97.

7 Report by David Bonavia in *The Times*, 20 November 1982.

8 For the strategic focus see the article by Chen Ziung, 'Where is the strategic focal point of the struggle for supremacy between the US and the USSR?', in *Beijing Shijie Zhishi* (World Knowledge), 10, 16 May 1981, pp.2–3, translated in *China Report, Foreign Broadcast Information Service*, (hereafter *FBIS*), *Political, Social and Military Affairs*, 212, 20 August 1981, pp.1–4.

9 Harry Harding, 'China and the Third World', in Solomon, pp.269–70.

10 'The importance of grasping the theory of the Three Worlds', reprinted from the *Norwegian Red Flag* by *Beijing Review*, xxi, 3, 20 January 1978, pp.23–4.

11 Harry Harding, 'China and the Third World', in Solomon, p.285.

12 *Beijing Review*, XXI, 9, 3 March 1978, p.22; for Huang Hua's speech, see *The Guardian* (Burma), 2 October 1980.

13 For discussion of the implications of the Peace Treaty of 1978 see Joseph Camilleri, *Chinese Foreign Policy: the Maoist era and its aftermath* (Oxford, 1980), p.214.

14 *The Times*, 16 July 1981.

15 Report by A. E. Collison from Tokyo in *The Times*, 27 February 1983.

16 *The Times*, 3 February and 9 February 1983.

17 *Beijing Review*, XXIII, 20, 19 May 1980, pp.6–7.

18 *International Herald Tribune*, 28 July 1982.

19 *The Times*, 15 February 1982.

20 See the report in the *Japan Times*, 17 October 1980, commenting on French President Giscard d'Estaing's call for a strong and independent Europe.

21 *Japan Times*, 22 June 1980.

22 Discussion of the 'development first' thesis, increasingly given priority since 1977, appears in Jonathon D. Pollak, 'China's Global Outlook and the Soviet Threat', in *Problems of Communism*, XXX, 1, pp.54–69.

23 David Bonavia in a despatch from Beijing in *The Times*, 12 November 1982: see also the report by Desmond Wettern in the *Daily Telegraph*, 13 November 1982.

24 *Newsweek*, 17 January 1983.

25 *The Times*, 20 October 1982.

26 *International Herald Tribune*, 5 August 1982.

27 Kyodo News Agency, 13 February 1982, noted in *SWB*, FE/6954.

28 For a development of this idea see Ann Fenwick, 'Chinese foreign policy and the campaign against Deng Xiaoping', in Thomas Fingar (ed.), *China's Quest for Independence: policy evolution in the 1970s* (Boulder, Colorado, 1980), pp.199–220.

29 References to this conflict are found in R. G. Sutter, *Chinese Foreign Policy after the Cultural Revolution, 1966–77* (Boulder, Colorado, 1978), pp.155–6.

30 Trade figures quoted appear in *Far Eastern Economic Review Asia Yearbook* (1977), p.159; for percentages of world trade see *Shijie Jingji Daobao*, 24 August 1981.

31 Chen Nai-ruenn, 'China's Foreign Trade, 1950–74', in *China: A Reassessment of the Economy: a compendium of papers submitted to the Joint Economic Committee, Congress of the United States* (Washington, DC, 1975), p.645.

32 Kyodo News Agency Report, 22 September 1981, in *SWB*, FE/ 6836.
33 Samuel Ho, 'The China Trade: recent developments and future prospects', in *Pacific Affairs*, 53, 2, Summer 1980, pp.269–89.
34 Japan External Trade Research Organization, *China Newsletter*, 37, March–April 1982, p.23.
35 *Time*, 31 January 1983.
36 *Newsweek*, 17 January 1983.
37 Percentages appear in the Communiqué on the Fulfilment of China's 1981 National Economic Plan, issued on 29 April 1982 by the State Statistical Bureau and published in *Beijing Review*, xxv, 20, 17 May 1982, pp.15–24.
38 The percentage of the 1970–78 period is given in Samuel Ho, 'The China Trade: recent developments and future prospects', in *Pacific Affairs*, 53, 2, Summer 1980 pp.269–89. The other percentages appear in *Beijing Review*, xxv, 2, 17 May 1982, pp.15–24.
39 *China Newsletter*, 35, November–December 1981, p.5.

2   Philosophical Infrastructure: Japan as mentor

1 Traditional Japanese social values are discussed in E. F. Vogel, 'Kinship Structure: migration to the city and modernisation' in R. P. Dore, *Aspects of Social Change in Modern Japan* (Princeton, NJ, 1967), p.106; see also Marius B. Jansen, *Changing Japanese Attitudes towards Modernisation* (Princeton, NJ, 1965), p.53.
2 An examination of commercial trends in the two societies appears in David S. Landes, 'Japan and Europe: contrasts in industrialisation', in W. W. Lockwood, *The State and Economic Enterprise in Japan* (Princeton, NJ, 1967), p.170.
3 For an examination of educational standards see E. W. Crawcour, 'The Tokugawa heritage', in Lockwood, p.35.
4 Relevant figures and details concerning types of school are to be found in H. Passin, 'Modernisation and the Japanese intellectual: some comparative observations', in Jansen, pp.454–5.
5 G. C. Allen, *Japan's Economic Policy*, (London, 1980), p.171.
6 David S. Landes in Lockwood, p.96.
7 For pursuit of this theme see Robert N. Bellah, 'Ienaga Saburo and the search for meaning in modern Japan' in Jansen, p.422.
8 Details of such funding are given in *Beijing Review*, xxii, 15, 13 April 1979, p.4; see also JETRO, *China Newsletter*, 44, May–June 1983, p.5.

9 *China Newsletter*, 40, September–October 1982, pp.2–3.

10 *China Newsletter*, 44, May–June, 1983, pp.13–17.

11 Such co-operation is emphasized in *Beijing Review*, XXII, 24, 15 June 1979.

12 *Beijing Review*, XXII, 17, 27 April 1979, p.19.

13 *China Newsletter*, 41, November–December 1982, p.5.

14 For an analysis of these unfavourable trends see Ivan D. London, Miriam London, and Ta-ling Lee, 'Prospects and dilemmas of Chinese workers', *Workers Under Communism*, 1, Spring 1982, pp.19–23.

15 Figures for Japan, the United States and the Soviet Union are from UNESCO sources.

16 *The Times Higher Education Supplement* (*THES*), 6 May 1983.

17 Such statistics are given in *Guangming Ribao GMRB*, 23 June 1983; projected enrolment figures appear in *GMRB*, 6 May 1983.

18 'Locally Run Universities Are One Way of Expanding Higher Education', (*GMRB*), 1 June 1983.

19 'The development of higher education must be speeded up', *GMRB*, 30 March 1983.

20 *GMRB*, 8 July 1983.

21 'Help progressive personnel enter universities', *GMRB*, 14 June 1983.

22 'How to select preferences for university enrolment examinations', *GMRB*, 6 June 1983.

23 For details see *Beijing Review*, XXII, 12, 23 March 1979, p.7.

24 *China Newsletter*, 44, May–June 1983, pp.13–17

3   China's Economic Strategy: The relevance of Japan's experience

1 For land tax figures, see the Epilogue in R. E. Ward (ed.), *Political Development in Modern Japan* (Princeton, NJ, 1968), pp.582–3; the question of the tax system is also discussed in K. Ohkawa and H. Rosovsky, 'A century of Japanese economic growth', in W. W. Lockwood, *The State and Economic Enterprise in Japan*, p.60. The importance of the primary sector was further evidenced by the composition of Japanese exports, with raw materials comprising 71 per cent of the total. This issue is raised by M. Kosaka, 'International economic policy', in R. A. Scalapino (ed.) *The Foreign Policy of Modern Japan*, pp.210–11.

2 K. Ohkawa and H. Rosovsky, 'A century of Japanese economic

growth', in Lockwood, p.88. See also David S. Landes, 'Japan and Europe: contrasts in industrialisation', in Lockwood, p.96.

3 Japan's pursuit of technological innovation is discussed by Thomas G. Rawski, *China's Transition to Industrialism* (Ann Arbor, Michigan, 1980), pp.151–2.

4 K. Ohkawa and H. Rosovsky in Lockwood, p.86.

5 W. W. Lockwood, 'Japan's New Capitalism', in Lockwood, p.459.

6 p.470.

7 p.467.

8 Economic controls during the Tokugawa period are discussed by E. S. Crawcour, 'The Tokugawa heritage', in Lockwood, pp.42–4.

9 See Rawski, *China's Transition to Industrialism*, (1980).

10 Thomas G. Rawski, 'The growth of producer industries', in Dwight Perkins, *China's Modern Economy in Historical Perspective* (Stanford, California, 1975), pp.203–33.

11 Rawski, *China's Transition to Industrialism*, pp.2–3.

12 Rawski in Perkins, pp.231–2.

13 *Beijing Review*, XXI, 49, 8 December 1978, p.15.

14 *Beijing Review*, XXI, 41, 13 October 1978, p.11.

15 For general reference see Nicholas R. Lardy, 'Economic planning and income distribution in China', *Current Scene*, XIV, 11, November 1976, p.6.

16 A. Watson, 'The management of the industrial economy: the return of the economists', in J. Gray and G. White (eds.), *China's New Development Strategy* (London, 1982), pp.87–118.

17 *China Business Review*, IX, 1, January–February 1982, pp.8–9.

18 *The Economist*, 12 March 1983.

19 *China Business Review*, IX, 1, January–February 1982, pp.8–9.

20 For coal output see *The Economist*, 12 March 1983.

21 Energy priorities are discussed in *China Business Review*, IX, 1, January–February 1982, pp.8–9.

22 Investment figures appear in *Beijing Review*, XXIII, 2, 14 January 1980, p.3.

23 Neville Maxwell, 'The Impact of China's New Economic Policies on the Rural Sector', in Gray and White, *China's New Development Strategy*, pp.256–8.

24 *The Times*, 14 April 1982.

25 *The Economist*, 12 March 1983.

26 Discussion of this question of capital for local heavy industry appears in J. Gray, 'Rural Enterprise in China, 1977–79', in

Gray and White, pp.223–4. Light industry's function is also given coverage in *Beijing Review*, xxii, 23, 8 January 1979, p.4.

27 *The Times*, 14 April 1982.

28 Investment percentages for light and heavy industry are given by Thierry Pairault, 'Industrial Strategy (January 1975 to June 1979): in search of new policies for industrial growth', in Gray and White, p.147.

29 *Beijing Review*, xxv, 22, 31 May 1982, pp.13–16.

30 Import duties are mentioned in the *Japan Times*, 27 April 1982 and the *BBC Economic Weekly*, 13 February 1982.

31 *SWB*, FE/W.1139, 24 June 1981.

32 For a discussion concerning the time-scale for the introduction of technology see *Beijing Review*, xxii, 22, 1 June 1979, p.10, and xxiii, 34, 25 August 1980, pp.23–5.

33 Details about the import of knowledge are provided by the *Chinese Business Review*, ix, 1, January–February 1982, pp.8–9; see also Shannon R. Brown, 'Foreign technology and economic growth', in *Problems of Communism*, July–August 1977, xxvi, 4, July–August 1977, pp.30–40.

34 Article by Robert Delfs in *The Times*, 22 April 1983; the above issues are also raised in *China Report, FBIS, Economic Affairs*, 156, 31 July 1981, pp.36–8.

35 Article by Jonathan Davis in *The Times*, 22 April 1983.

36 Broadcast by Tianjin City Radio, 14 February 1981, in *SWB*, FE/W.1125.

37 For output percentages see *China Newsletter*, 31, March–April 1981, p.25, and 32, May–June 1981, p.23. Future projections are considered by Jonathan Davis in *The Times*, 22 April 1983.

38 Growth rates for the light and heavy industrial sectors in 1979 appear in *Beijing Review*, xxiii, 20, 19 May 1980, pp.17–19; figures for 1980 are to be found in *China Newsletter*, 33, July – August 1981, p.3. 1982 statistics are cited by Robert Delfs in *The Times*, 22 April 1983. See also *The Economist*, 12 March 1983, p.71.

39 For a discussion of these factors see *The Economist*, 12 March 1983.

40 D. Bonavia in *The Times*, 22 April 1983.

41 Article by Graham Johnson in *The Times*, 22 April 1983.

42 The 1978 and 1979 figures appear in *China Newsletter*, No. 35, November–December 1981, p.10; those for 1981 and 1982 are given in *The Economist*, 12 March 1983, p.71.

43 *Beijing Review*, xxiv, 28, 13 July 1981, p.6.

44 *New China News Agency* (hereafter *NCNA*) broadcast in English, 9 January 1981, as reported in *SWB*.
45 *SWB*, FE/W.1141, 8 July 1981.
46 For development of this idea see A. Watson in Gray and White, p.118.
47 Deng, in his statement about the colour of the cat, implied that in the economic field efficiency should be the main criterion. Thus private farming and market forces in industry are all right if they raise production. For reference to this issue see J. B. Starr, 'From the Tenth Party Congress to the Premiership of Hua Guofeng', in *China Quarterly*, 67, September 1976, p.477. The relationship between central planning and the market is discussed in *Beijing Review*, XXIII, 12, 24 March 1980, p.25.
48 These changes are examined by A. Watson in Gray and White, p.107.
49 *The Economist*, 12 March 1983.
50 *The Times*, 14 March 1982.
51 These issues are discussed by J. Gray in Gray and White, p.291, and Neville Maxwell, 'The Impact of China's New Policies in the Rural Sector', p.259.
52 For a detailed analysis of these questions see Mitch Meisner and Marc Blecher, 'Administrative level and agrarian structure, 1975–80: the county as focal point in Chinese rural development policy', in Gray and White, p.77, and J. Gray, p.233.

4 Sino-Japanese Partnership: Trade and economic co-operation

1 *Beijing Review*, XXII, 14, 6 April 1979, p.31.
2 For the Council's role, see XXII, 17, 27 April 1979, pp.20–22.
3 These problems are discussed in a report in *SWB*, FE/7073, 9 July 1982.
4 See *China Newsletter*, 41, November–December 1982, p.16.
5 The 1978 coal agreement is mentioned in *SWB*, FE/6671, 12 March 1981; details of the Export-Import Bank loans appear in *SWB*, FE/W.1143, 22 July 1981.
6 Such terms are listed in *China Newsletter*, 35, November–December 1981.
7 For a discussion of this theme see 40, September–October 1982, pp.18–23.
8 *SWB*, FE/W.1132, 6 May 1981.

9 For details see Zhao Suzheng, 'What taxes should foreigners pay in China?' *Beijing Review*, xxiv, 43, 29 October 1981, pp.20–21.

10 Relevant information is given in *China Newsletter*, 32, May–June 1981, pp.26–7.

11 These conditions are outlined in 'Regulations of the People's Republic of China on the exploitation of offshore petroleum reserves in co-operation with foreign enterprises', *Beijing Review*, xxv, 8, 22 February 1982, pp.14–18; see also xxiv, 16, 20 April 1981, pp.15–20.

12 *SWB*, FE/W.1131, 29 April 1981.

13 FE/W.1196, 4 August 1982.

14 A broadcast from Fujian, 8 June 1981, in FE/W.1140, 1 July 1981.

15 *China Newsletter*, 36, January–February 1982, p.24.

16 The theoretical and practical problems involved in developing Special Economic Zones were discussed in the Chinese journal *Shijie Jingji Daobao*, 37, 15 June 1981, as reported in *SWB*, FE/6785, 27 July 1981.

17 *Beijing Review*, xxiii, 40, 6 October 1980, pp.20–21.

18 *SWB*, FE/6958, 19 February 1982.

19 For details of development in the Special Economic Zones see Simon Scott Plummer, 'Letter from Shenzhen', *The Times*, 20 August 1982; further discussion appears in 'Leaky Capitalist Enclaves', *The Economist*, 22 November 1982. The possibility of a southern economic zone is examined in an article by Graham Earnshaw in the *Daily Telegraph*, 1 August 1983.

20 Sadako Ogata, 'The Business Community and Japanese Foreign Policy: Normalisation of relations with the People's Republic of China', in Robert A. Scalapino (ed.), *The Foreign Policy of Modern Japan*, p.178.

21 For these trade figures see *The Times*, 27 September 1982.

22 The figure for 1983 appears in the *Bulletin*, 5 April 1983; that for 1980 is given in *SWB*, FE/W.1126, 25 March 1981.

23 *SWB*, FE/W.1126, 25 March 1981.

24 *Newsweek*, 9 May 1983.

25 *The Times*, 19 October 1982.

26 *SWB*, FE/W.1179, 7 April 1982.

27 See a New China News Agency report quoted in *SWB*, FE/W.1138, 10 June 1981.

28 *China Newsletter*, 41, November–December 1982, p.13.

29 *Beijing Review*, xxii, 33, 17 August 1979, p.27.

30 Details appear in *China Newsletter*, 43, March–April 1983, p.23.
31 *Ibid.*

5 Conclusions: Towards a Sino-Japanese Axis

1 These trends in Chinese foreign policy are examined at length in an article by Tatsume Okabe, 'Chinese diplomacy as reflected at the recent National People's Congress', *China Newsletter*, 47, November–December 1983, pp.2–6.
2 *China Newsletter*, 48, January–February 1984, p.1.
3 For bilateral trade figures see *SWB*, FE/W.1271, 25 January 1984; specific details concerning China's oil and coal sales appear in *China Newsletter*, 47, November–December 1983, p.21. Oil production statistics and reserves are also mentioned in *SWB*, FE/W.1272, 1 February 1984.
4 Details of this survey are given in *China Newsletter*, 48, January–February 1984, p.24.
5 *SWB*, FE/7557, 3 February 1984.
6 For discussion of entrenched vested interests by the Chinese Communist Press see, for example, 'Progress curbed by protecting the backward', *Renmin Ribao*, 10 January 1984.
7 A brief examination of the White Paper appears in *The Times*, 27 August 1983.
8 *SWB*, FE/7539, 13 January 1984.

Suggestions for further reading

General background

Beasley, W. G., *The Modern History of Japan*, 2nd edn (Weidenfeld & Nicolson, 1973). An excellent study of modern Japan.
Beckmann, George M., *The Modernization of China and Japan* (Harper & Row, 1962). A useful comparative focus.
Clubb, O. Edmund, *20th Century China*, 3rd edn (Columbia University Press, 1978). A wide-ranging historical perspective.

Contemporary political institutions

Pempel, T. J., *Policy and Politics in Japan* (Temple University Press, 1982). An original approach to policies and issues.
Townsend, James R., *Politics in China*, 2nd edn (Little, Brown, 1980). A comprehensive treatment of government policies and processes.
Waller, D. J., *The Government and Politics of the People's Republic of China* (Hutchinson, 1981). A concise analysis of China's political system.
Ward, Robert E., *Japan's Political System*, 2nd edn (Prentice-Hall, 1978). A detailed examination of Japanese political parties and governmental performance.

Foreign policy

Kahn, Herman, *The Emerging Japanese Superstate* (Penguin Books, 1973). Some stimulating ideas concerning Japan's present and future.
Mancall, M., *China at the Center* (Free Press, 1984). China's foreign relations placed in an historical setting.
Scalapino, Robert A., ed., *The Foreign Policy of Modern Japan* (Univer-

sity of California Press, 1977). Especially useful for study of institutional mechanisms of Japanese foreign policy decision-making.

Solomon, Richard H., ed., *The China Factor* (Prentice-Hall, 1981). Full coverage of China's relations with major states.

Economic development

Allen, G. C., *The Japanese Economy* (Weidenfeld & Nicolson, 1981). Easy to follow guide to Japan's post-war economy.

Barnett, A. D., *China's Economy in Global Perspective* (Brookings Institution, 1981). Examines China's modernisation programme and world trade.

Donnithorne, A., *China's Economic System* (Allen & Unwin, 1967). Pre-dates the current development programme but is a detailed study of China's post-1949 economic institutions.

Dore, R. P., ed., *Aspects of Social Change in Modern Japan* (Princeton University Press, 1967). Discusses the social values underpinning the modernisation process.

Gray, Jack and White, Gordon, eds., *China's New Development Stategy* (Academic Press, 1982). Assesses present economic policies.

Lockwood, W. W., *The State and Economic Enterprise in Japan* (Princeton University Press, 1965). A broad view of Japan's modern economy.

Ohkawa K. and Rosovsky H., *Japanese Economic Growth* (Stanford University Press, 1973). A comprehensive survey of Japan's economic development.

Perkins, Dwight H., *China's Modern Economy in Historical Perspective* (Stanford University Press, 1975). A useful background to the Chinese leaders' economic policies.

Business

Wik, Philip, *How to do Business with the People's Republic of China* (Reston Publishing Co. Inc., 1984).

Index

Academy of Sciences, 37–8
ASEAN, 17
Asia and the Pacific, 5, 8, 10–11, 110, 116
See also Southeast Asia
Asian Development Bank, 115
Asian-African Problems Research Association, 4

Bank of China, 75, 76, 79, 82
Beijing, 72, 78, 79, 80–81, 92, 93, 103
Beijing Electromechanical Company Limited, 84
Beijing Review, 9, 12, 50, 59, 64, 87
Beijing Television Factory, 93

Chen Yun, 53
Chiang Kai-shek, 1, 4
China: agricultural development and reform, 19–20, 36, 42, 44, 49, 52, 56, 59, 63–4, 69, 78, 94; border disputes, 2, 3, 8, 9, 12, 48, 88–9, 96–7, 99; cultural and social development, 19, 23, 24, 31–2, 35–8, 40–41, 44, 46, 53, 56–7, 63–4, 66, 85, 86, 105–06, 108; defence policy, 9–11, 13–15, 17, 31, 100, 112, 115; dependency on the West, 18–19, 37–8, 50, 53, 59–60; economic development, 17–18, 23–4, 32–6, 40–42, 47–70, 72–3, 85–9, 94, 101–03, 104, 107. *See also* foreign investment in; education, 24, 31, 36, 37–42, 108, 109; exports, 19, 59, 61, 64–5, 72–3, 79–80, 87; foreign policy, 5–11, 96–100, 112; foreign trade, 18–19, 33, 49, 52, 54, 58–60, 64–5, 71–4, 99, 104; imports, 19–21, 56, 58, 59–60, 64, 65, 93, 101–03; industrial development, 34, 47, 48, 50, 51–8, 60–69, 72–83, 86, 88, 101, 103; oil production and export, 55–6, 61–2, 76, 82–3, 88, 92–3, 102; technological and scientific development, 23, 36, 38, 39, 40–41, 48, 50, 93. *See also* Sino-Japanese relations.
China Council for the Promotion of International Trade, 73
China International Trust and Investment Corporation, 73, 81, 84
China Machinery Import and Export Corporation, 72, 78
China National Import and Export Commodities Inspection Corporation, 73
China National Offshore Oil Corporation (CNOOC), 83
China Orient Leasing Company Ltd, 84
China Textile Import and Export Corporation, 80
Chinese Communist Party (CCP), 1, 33, 36–7, 40–41, 42, 48, 50–51, 66, 85, 106–07; economic